That Little Hug At The End

Correspondence with a Bank Robber

by
R. Dwight Laws, Ph.D

Bloomington, IN  Milton Keynes, UK

authorHOUSE™

AuthorHouse™
1663 Liberty Drive, Suite 200
Bloomington, IN 47403
www.authorhouse.com
Phone: 1-800-839-8640

AuthorHouse™ UK Ltd.
500 Avebury Boulevard
Central Milton Keynes, MK9 2BE
www.authorhouse.co.uk
Phone: 08001974150

First published by AuthorHouse 4/9/2007

ISBN: 978-1-4259-9928-5 (sc)

Library of Congress Control Number: 2007902094

Printed in the United States of America
Bloomington, Indiana

This book is printed on acid-free paper.

Cover design by Greg Thomas.

Editing by Theda Timmins.

FORWARD

I work in an office where we do distance education via correspondence and also via the internet. One day my secretary brought me a letter with the return address of the Lompoc Penitentiary in California. The inmate had registered for one of our courses and had sent a letter of inquiry about the course content. I read the letter and was somewhat taken back.

"What is this guy doing in prison?" I thought. His writing and thinking skills are excellent.

On the spot, and for no logical reason I can think of, I got the idea it might be fun to strike up a correspondence with an inmate.

I found it curious I was jittery when I wrote the first letter; not unlike my first phone call to a girlfriend.

It turned out to be so successful I started writing to more and more convicts. At one time I was corresponding with twelve different inmates, including a woman, a double murderer, a bank robber, a husband killer, a murderer, a chronic repeat offender, two wife abusers, and five others who never would tell me why they were in (and after corresponding with them and getting to know their personalities I really didn't want to know).

One inmate mistook my name to be female and I promptly received a package full of shopping coupons and a self-created love poem. He also sent me a lovable drawing (he was very good) of Donald and Daisy Duck smooching on the beach. I'm not sure why he sent that? Maybe a woman would know. When I told him he had the wrong gender he wrote back an apology and although he was embarrassed we continued the correspondence. I was glad he kept writing because his insights and opinions about one state's prison system were insightful to me – if not terrifying.

Some of my *pen pals* (Sorry! I couldn't resist such a wonderful opportunity) became close enough to me I visited them in prison. I visited the double murderer in Connecticut, the repeat offender in Colorado, Mike (who this book is about) in Phoenix and again when he was transferred to Tucson.

My sweetest letters came from the young woman in New Jersey. She was released while we were writing and I never heard from her again. My bitterest letter was smoldering when I opened the envelope. I wrote back and told that inmate we must conclude our letter writing unless he stopped swearing and using filthy language. I knew it might end there because I was sure he would be incapable of writing a complete sentence without using his favorite words. He surprised me by cleaning up his act and actually showing great creativity in his writing and thinking thereafter.

A very intriguing experience was getting a letter from a woman who held a masters degree from Michigan State and a Ph.D. from the University of Southern California. She had just completed her 22nd year in prison. She wrote, "I am an inmate in the world's largest prison for women—and also, I might add—the world's most violent. We have a record number of assaults, including stabbings, gang beatings, rapes and other forms of violence; and a record number of prisoner-on-prisoner murders." I looked into this one a little more and discovered she was in jail for putting a contract out to have her husband murdered. The contract was with a corrupt segment of the police department in her city. They killed her husband. Amazing.

Most of the inmates claimed I was their ONLY contact with the outside. That made me a little nervous. "Don't tell them which city we live in," my wife begged me. It was emotional to see how they clung to me and panicked if they thought I might stop writing. To protect myself from being overwhelmed with the correspondence I set a rule I would write one month and they would respond the next. That meant six letters a year to each inmate. Twelve times six still turned out to be a huge task (72 letters each year).

During my visit to Connecticut I sat in a highly secure waiting room staring into the face of a very hard-looking black woman who was obviously there to visit an inmate. We waited and waited and then I overheard her mumbling she wondered when she would get to visit Dennis her son (fictitious name).

"Are you Dennis' mother?" I bravely asked her.

With somewhat of a surprised look she said, "Yes."

She probably wondered why the only white guy in the visiting room was talking to her.

"I'm here to visit Dennis as well," I said.

"Oh! Are you the man Dennis has been telling me about who is a college professor that writes to him and is riding a motorcycle all the way from Utah to visit him?"

"Yes. That's me."

Her hard look disappeared and she rushed at me with a radiant smile and hugged me and kissed me and wept tears and praised Jesus over and over again. She was a large women and I had never before experience such smothering love.

Later while we were visiting Dennis she dominated the conversation. My visit to Dennis turned out to be only a side bar.

"Dennis is such a good boy but he is too much like his Daddy." She rolled her eyes as she mentioned Daddy.

"They put him away for life. That just isn't fair. They were too harsh on his sentence," she sobbed.

"They treated me like I had done something worse than killing the President of the United States," Dennis said. "I guess I did – I killed two white guys."

"But they deserved it dear," she consoled.

Dennis must have seen the question mark on my face and he offered an explanation. "They were raping my sister when I caught them."

Afterward, in the parking lot Dennis' mother told me a story of a sad life with an abusive husband, Dennis' Daddy. She praised me endlessly for coming to visit her good boy. As I rode away I think I was in a mild state of shock from the whole experience.

Other equally fascinating experiences occurred from writing letters to inmates. One inmate took great pains to try and convert me to Buddhism. Another asked me to get a picture of the San Diego Mormon Temple when I told him my youngest son was going to be married there. He was an atheist but said he had seen that building and it was the most beautiful in the world. Just before the wedding a package arrived from that inmate. It was a colored pencil drawing (the only implements he was allowed because he is serving his time in solitary) of the San Diego Temple. It was amazingly beautiful. We framed it and displayed it at the reception.

These various prisoners each expressed love and concern in their letters when they learned I was fighting cancer. Their words were as tender as a loving sibling and their concerns were real. I'm sure they would never let a fellow 'cellie' read such tender statements. But in the secrecy of a personal letter even these hard, sometimes vicious, inmates had a soft center. Others were afraid to express sentiment. "I will not express my true feelings because my letters are read by the guards and will come back on me as a mockery," one inmate expressed.

This book, however, is about only one of the inmates, Mike Taylor. His amazing story will bring tears. You will have to read on to find out what kind of tears.

Throughout this book you will see "* * * * * * * *". This is to spare you the many lines of general "how's the weather" comments. We discussed our families and other subjects at great length. I left out most of our correspondence and used the "* * * * * * * *" as an indicator of missing text. The text I left in is word for word from our correspondence.

From time to time I also use [. . .] brackets to insert an explanatory statement or thought that was not part of the original correspondence.

During all our years of correspondence, Mike wrote hand written letters on a yellow legal size lined paper using a ball point pen.

Meet Mike Taylor: Bank Robber

"I knew it was going to end soon. You can feel them closing in."

I had a '69 Coup de Ville all terrain Cadillac, a sawed-off Mossberg pump shot-gun, a handgun, a black cowboy hat, Levis, cowboy boots, and the stereo blasting "I Can Feel it in the Air" by Phil Collins. Over and over and over again, I played that song as I checked my weapons. Shotgun loaded. Check. Handgun loaded. Check. I had been drinking too. Heavily. And just to "take the edge off," I was eating 10 mg Valiums like they were candy. I cannot even begin to imagine a more deadly combination than that.

* * * * * * * *

An IROC pulls out behind me. Keeping their distance as the vans approach. It's the S.W.A.T. team that was lying in wait for me at the deserted concrete factory. They were called in for the kill.

One last chance. I knew it too. If she didn't start this time, it was over.

"C'mon Baby. . .please. . ." I rubbed the dashboard. Turned the key. She fired up! It was on! The chase was on! I left 'em in a cloud of black smoke!

* * * * * * * *

I made a few more evasive maneuvers to no avail. This is when the Coup de Ville became an all-terrain-vehicle. I was watching my mirror trying to establish the whereabouts of that blue dot. When I looked up, it was too late. The road made a 90 degree turn. I went straight through an iron gate into a field. Never slowed down.

Now I remember running parallel to a fence through a pasture. I had to get on the other side. The grass is always greener, right? I went through the fence, the long way, puncturing my radiator with a fence post. Back onto a road with barbed wire wrapped around my left front tire.

It was an awesome sight to behold. They said I did this seven times. I don't remember. All I remember is those two white vans.

* * * * * * * *

Don't know how long I was out but started dreaming. I heard my name being called way off in the distance somewhere. "Mike. . .Mike. . ."

I didn't want to be disturbed.

"Mike. . .It's over. . .Don't make me kill you. . ."

"Don't make us kill you Mike!!!"

Mike Taylor: #85227-011
Lompoc Penitentiary, California

"I have never done this before and must confess that I am a little nervous about the prospects of trying to invite myself into someone else's life."

June 16, 1995

Dear Michael:

I am the Director of the Department of Independent Study at Brigham Young University. It came to my attention you have applied for a partial scholarship with our department. Although I am aware of all such requests I do not sit on the committee that reviews and approves them. Hence, I do not know if your request was accepted or denied. So what is the purpose of this letter? I was wondering if you would be interested in having a correspondence with me.

My activities are numerous and I am very busy but I think I would find it enjoyable and fulfilling to strike up a monthly communication with you. I know it is presumptuous on my part to make such a request since we don't know each other. Of course I will not be offended if you find this inquiry a little bizarre and choose not to accept my proposal.

* * * * * * * *

I am a private pilot, a licensed scuba diver, an avid fan of basketball, a former member of the Tabernacle Choir, and a current motorcycle enthusiast. I have biked on my Kawasaki 1500 through all of the Canadian Provinces, all of the western U.S., and all of New England. I am also a family man. This is probably enough to say about myself, at least until I know if you are interested in communicating with me.

Sincerely,
R. Dwight Laws

First Response:
The Beginning of a Friendship

"The judge has given me twelve years and five months to think it over. Of course with good behavior, I can be out in ten. Five down, five to go."

During all our years of correspondence, Mike wrote hand-written letters on a yellow legal size lined paper using a ball-point pen.

July 24, 1995

Dear Mr. Laws:

I have put a great deal of thought into your letter that I have read over and over <u>many</u> times. And I would consider it a <u>great</u> honor and privilege to correspond with you on a personal basis.

However, I must warn you my letters at times may seem somewhat boring and redundant. Please allow me to explain. It has to do with a tightly controlled environment. Rather repetitious at times in other words.

Although there's always something happening inside these walls, I'm not always permitted to talk about it. It's O.K. to look around as long as you don't actually "see" anything, or say anything! Believe me, I've seen enough in five years to last me a lifetime.

My only regret is I cannot keep a journal. There's no doubt it would be a best seller someday.

* * * * * * * *

So how did I end up in a maximum security federal penitentiary?

In an "unscrupulous pursuit of selfish ends through evil means. . ."(I borrowed that from Nathaniel Hawthorne's "House of the Seven Gables". ALSO "BORROWED" SOME MONEY FROM THE WRONG BANK!

* * * * * * * *

I'll be out sometime in the year 2001. Starting over at the age of 41, in 2001! Sounds scary, doesn't it? This is why I need to change my ways. I get one more chance, that's it. And there's still so much to do!

* * * * * * *

Mom said, "That in a moment of weakness Michael robbed those banks. . ." Bless her heart! Little does she know how many "moments of weakness" I had!

They convicted me on six. That's enough to hold me awhile.

* * * * * * *

Now, I am not bragging, nor am I proud of what I have done. But there is a certain thrill to robbing banks.

* * * * * * *

I was raised proper. My family still stands behind me today. Don't know what I would have done without them. Worked all my life. Was taught family values throughout. My attitude had a lot to do with it. When I was fifteen, I knew <u>everything</u>. This is not the first time I've been in trouble either. This time they got my attention though.

There's more. But I'm not going to try and put it all into one letter.

I too was a little nervous at first. Thank you for being patient. And I truly hope we can continue this correspondence. In fact, I was somewhat flattered someone of your caliber would even take an interest in me.

Take care and I hope to hear from you soon.

Respectfully,

Michael

Second Correspondence

"Is hate still taking up space in your thinking processes? Are you offended if I talk to you about personal things, such as your family and your god?"

August 16, 1995

Dear Mike:

It was a pleasant surprise to hear your response. I am pleased you are willing to carry on this correspondence. Thank you for sharing some of your feelings and telling me briefly of your situation. You write very well and your writing tells me you have deep and complex thought processes. This is encouraging to me because I am of the opinion a meaningful correspondence will require more than discussions about the weather and fault-finding to boost ones own ego. A worthwhile interchange, it seems to me, would include politics, sports, family, education, economics, world affairs and spirituality.

* * * * * * * *

Since I intend an extended interchange with you I won't try to tell all about myself in one letter. However, here is a little more information. My wife, Linda, and I have nine children (seven sons, and two daughters) and twenty grandchildren. We tried to raise them in the precepts of the restored gospel. We taught them many of the same things you experienced in your home. We have had some very satisfying results and also some bitter disappointments.

I ask myself, why do my offspring do such wonderful things that inspire and fill my soul with joy, and then turn around and do something that causes my soul grief? Perhaps this is part of my training as an aspiring creator myself. I need to understand the concepts of justice and mercy more clearly.

* * * * * * * *

The beauty of the plan of salvation, wrought by the atonement of Christ, is that you can be as worthy, clean and pure as the guy standing next to you at the judgment bar, even if he never committed any robberies. If you reach out and grasp that process you can be completely without scar or debt. Wonderful, isn't it?

* * * * * * *

My plan is to write you on the 16th of every other month. Hopefully, that will be often enough to be enjoyable to you and not so often as to cause you to grow weary of it. That also gives you a few weeks to respond between each letter. It also sets your expectations--you don't have to wonder if I am going to write, or when.

Sincerely,
Dwight

P.S. Please address me as Dwight and not Dr. Laws. I only use that title in stuffy faculty settings or at formal seminars where we go around patting each other on the back and self congratulating ourselves for some nebulous research achievement which no one really cares about.

Dwight, I'm Really Enjoying This Correspondence

"Of course, around here, it's not wise to get too relaxed. Twice I have walked right into 'situations' for not being keenly aware and alert. Both situations were vicious, brutal stabbings. Not a pretty sight."

Sept. 6, 1995

Dear Dwight:

September sixth <u>already</u>! Wow! Time flies when your havin'fun, doesn't it? (Har! Har!)

It's what you make of it, I guess is what counts. "Even in chains a man is <u>free</u> to make something out of what has been made of him." Had to resort to my chrestomathy for that one. Don't know who said it, but I sure do like it.

Sometimes it's extremely difficult to keep a positive attitude in this environment, but some good things have been happening lately. Your letters, for example, are some really good <u>positive</u> input for me.

* * * * * * * *

I feel comfortable with this arrangement, which is unlike me. For I usually guard my true feelings closely. But for some reason, I feel as though I need not hide anything from you. I trust you completely and do not mind you sharing these letters with your wife, Linda, and your close friends. In fact, I'm somewhat flattered that anyone would even care about someone on this side of these fences.

* * * * * * * *

I can watch the sunrise. I think I may have mentioned this previously. It is peaceful. And upon rare occasions, (three times in the past five years), I have caught a glimpse of the stars! But you must be quick.

Quicker than the emergency generator back-up system! When the lights kick back on, the stars fade away. . . But for a few precious moments, the view is spectacular.

* * * * * * *

Have I let someone down? Numerous times. I'll tell you why. Drugs became the most important thing in my life. I was way beyond the experimental stage. When you are an "extremist" with an "addictive personality," it becomes frightening how you can let something like that control your life. And how easily you get out of control when <u>nothing</u> else matters.

* * * * * * *

I want to elaborate on "unconditional love" and "hatred" next letter. 'Til then, take care!

Sincerely,
Mike

Stars

"Maybe the glimpses of Heaven are more entic-
ing than a full blown presentation."

October 16, 1995

Dear Mike:

Your experience of glimpsing the stars for just a brief moment before the backup generator kicks in has some powerful and thought provoking metaphorical elements. For example, I have had occasions when I thought I had a brief glimpse of eternity. Sometimes in meetings I have been elevated to a feeling of euphoric love and appreciation for my fellowmen. But like your experience, the feeling passes in a few seconds and I am back to mortality. I get these glimpses when I am holding my new grandbabies. I get it when a young person in our stake gives a particularly humble and sweet testimony. I get it when I hear the prophets speak. But, like the stars in your prison, they are only glimpses and then I sit with a melancholy feeling and wish I could sustain the feeling for much longer periods. Maybe Heavenly Father wants it that way. You undoubtedly have an appreciation for the stars I don't have.

* * * * * * * *

The article you sent from the New Yorker, "Teaching Prisoners A Lesson" was very sobering. I read it several times. Quotes from prisoners about being in prison before ever being locked up was a frightening commentary on the grip Satan has on the world. The "Chains of Hell" are already wrapped around so many and they threaten each of us daily, whereever we may be. The article didn't give a lot of hope for many incarcerated individuals. It doesn't appear public opinion about the treatment of prisoners is very forgiving does it? They seem determined to have justice but have lost track of the mercy elements.

* * * * * * * *

You mentioned your drugs. Let me tell you of an exhilarating "high" I had a few weeks ago. I was watching on TV a youth orchestra and chorus performing a number called "Come Thou Fount of Every Blessing". These weren't kids that were into sin, drugs, gangs, sex, and crimes against society. They were kids who were declaring they wanted God to take their hearts and seal it to Himself. It was tremendous. As the number proceeded to a climax the camera zeroed in on several faces. At the precise moment the orchestra was booming out a crescendo and the youth were singing the phrase "Here's my heart, O take and seal it", and the camera was on the face of a young woman who was singing with all her heart, a tear fell from her eye and ran down her cheek. My heart exploded and instantly tears ran down my cheeks as well. Mike, can you imagine such a feeling? Another glimpse of the stars?

* * * * * * *

You will hear from me again in a couple of months as per the arranged schedule. God bless you and let you know He is aware of you. I am also aware of you but I cannot come into your cell. He can.

Dwight

Too Much?

"I am somewhat concerned!"

To the reader: At this point in our correspondence there was a misunderstanding. A few days before receiving this letter in the mail I had sent out my next letter. This little letter tore me up inside.

October 10, 1995

Dear Dwight:

I didn't hear from you last month. I hope that all is well? Perhaps my last letter was too much all at once? Or maybe something happened to the mail. I am hoping that you have not chosen to discontinue our correspondence. If this is the case, would you tell me? Believe me, I would understand.

* * * * * * * *

Please let me know what's happening.

Sincerely,
Mike

Prison Riot of '95

*"It all started over dessert. One guy want-
ed another's dessert. Bad timing!"*

November 27, 1995

Dear Dwight:

Obviously, I am not as well organized as you. Otherwise I would've
known there was no need for panic after all. (I got your letter)

* * * * * * *

First of all, a brief update of what's been happening in "paradise." (Do
you detect a tone of irony in the air?)

* * * * * * *

The entire federal prison system was locked down nationwide as a
precautionary measure due to some uprisings on the east coast. The
Supreme Court upheld its original ruling on some drug laws. Namely,
crack-cocaine. Predominately a black drug. So the Blacks naturally scream
"racism," and start burning down the joints in retaliation.

* * * * * * *

Our third or fourth day here, of the lockdown, they try a "controlled
feed." That is, one cell-block at a time. This is the worst possible time and
place to start any trouble of any kind. Believe me, they were ready. And
they lost control.

A fist fight erupted between an inmate and a guard over a dessert issue.
That was the spark that ignited the pandemonium! Wayne movies where
they're having a bar-room brawl? Well, that's what it looked like!

When those of us who were smart enough to get out of the way
were marched past K, L, & M units, single file, in restraints, it triggered
something. Could this be what Carl Jung referred to as the "collective
unconscious?"

* * * * * * *

Peace was restored with violence, tear gas, percussion grenades and intimidation. Within two weeks, all was quiet, once again, on the Western Front.

* * * * * * * *

My son, Jacob, just turned 18. We had a nice long chat on his birthday. We're not as close as I'd like to be, but that's my fault. After all, he's not the one who ran off and left me! His mother and I were never married but are still best friends, so that helps too. We were high-school sweethearts, so some feelings have never diminished. Even though she is now married, and I respect that, my love for her is UN-CONDITIONAL.

My daughter is one I've never met. She's nineteen now. We've spoken on occasion and corresponded through the mail. She's pretty wild. Jake (my son) and she have met, just recently in fact.

Her [Amanda, my daughter] mother was murdered in 1990. I had just started my bankrobbing spree. The murder was so brutal that I am going to spare you the details. [note: I learned a few years later when I visited Mike that she was stabbed in the throat and ripped open to down below her navel]. How can you possibly not hate somebody who can do something like that? Especially if he has priors? And was set free to kill again? And then was set free again due to a technicality! Am I supposed to love *something* like that?

* * * * * * * *

I want to elaborate some more on "unconditional love" and "hatred." I feel I have just skimmed the surface, and do not want to cut you short – maybe next letter.

That was a touching story about the video. I will work on the words of the song and send an essay of the meaning, as I see it.

* * * * * * * *

The picture is a fine picture. You have a lot to be proud of. I showed it to an "acquaintance" of mine, and he said, "Wow! That guy can have his own baseball team!"

* * * * * * * *

I will probably read your letter several more times and reflect upon it some more. Each time I read through it, I find something else that I would like to comment on.

If by chance you do not hear from me by Christmas, please have a very Merry One!

Sincerely,
Mike

The Family Teams

"The Creator does not have a "collective unconscious". He is aware of even the sparrow that falls to the ground."

December 15, 1995

Dear Mike:

Merry Christmas and a Happy New Year! I am particularly glad you were safe during the riot. I can't imagine such an environment. I suppose the "collective unconscious", which you are presently a member of, is all too real. Fortunately, our Creator is definitely aware of you and me. He knows our names. He is not full of hatred. That is the message of this season.

* * * * * * *

Tell your friend that my family has actually played as a baseball team. Last summer we entered a co-ed league. The rules require every other batter be female and every team field five men and five women (slow-pitch softball). Linda and I, along with our children and their spouses did very well and came in second in the league. In the last game Linda was chasing a fly ball in right field. She stumbled and fell. She complained her ankle hurt so we told her it was okay to just sit in right field. We couldn't let her leave the game because we would forfeit (we had no substitutes that particular game). So she sat down and we finished the game with a victory. Afterward we went and patted her on the shoulder and told her "Good job, Mom. You helped us win the game just by sitting there". We laughed, she laughed, and we all had a good time over a hamburger at JB's. The next morning at the doctor's office we discovered she had a broken leg. Suddenly we were all feeling terrible we had been so insensitive to her problem. Winning seemed to become more important to us than her welfare. Of course we didn't realize how serious it was but we were sobered nevertheless.

* * * * * * *

One more quick story. One day while I was playing with four of my sons at the BYU fieldhouse, we got into a pickup game and there was some intense competition. One of the opposing team members, who didn't know we were family, was pushing and fouling my smallest son, unnecessarily. I finally said, "Hey, take it easy on the kid. This isn't for the world championship you know." The big burly guy turned to me, butt his nose in my face and said with a sneer, "What's it to you grandpa? You act like he is your kid, or something". I responded, "they are *all* my kids". He turned and looked at three other big strong guys who had heard his "grandpa" remark. They weren't smiling at him. Later we all sat at Wendy's piggin' out on french fries and laughing as we recalled the look on the guy's face.

* * * * * * *

God bless you, especially at this time of the year. May he give you solace and peace, which bars cannot keep out.

Dwight.

Bed of Roses

"It's well worth getting up early just to savor the silence."

January 30, 1996

Dear Dwight:

I was up early, when all was quiet. So quiet, you could hear a "rose blooming on a boundless, snow-covered plain of silence. . ." Isn't that beautiful? I wrote that down in my chrestomathy awhile back, but failed to record the author! Shame on me!

* * * * * * * *

I like the "message of this season." Believe me, it's going to be a real challenge. Something to really work towards. It's so easy to find fault in others, but someone explained to me that when one is being captious, all he's doing is finding the fault in himself. Perhaps it would be better to start looking for the <u>good</u> instead.

* * * * * * * *

Mom is a strong advocate of free choice. We all have the capability of choosing right from wrong. That's why you will <u>never</u> hear me complaining about my "bed of roses." I have accepted responsibility for my actions and must now deal with it. And am starting to believe there's someone else we must <u>all</u> answer to.

* * * * * * * *

This correspondence has been fabulous for me too. It gives me a lot to think about. The positive input has been extremely beneficial for me.

* * * * * * * *

I thoroughly enjoyed the stories about your family's baseball and basketball adventures. Both have a moral. And I particularly like the way you shut that big bully up on the basketball court! That one's a classic! That's one you can tell your grandkids about. And they can pass it on down through the generations to come. Adding just a little to it each time.

* * * * * * *

"Til then, as they say down in Texas, "ya'll take real good care." And I am looking forward to your next letter.

Sincerely,
<u>Mike</u>

Prisons of a Multiple Kind

"He is, by his own admission, a prisoner of his passions."

February 16, 1996

Dear Mike:

I enjoyed reading your last letter. I find myself looking forward to them when that time of the month approaches. When I thumb through my mountain of mail and see your letter I stop immediately, open and read it, before going on.

* * * * * * * *

Today I wanted to share with you a letter I recently received. This internet student was responding to an assignment to tell the faculty member a little bit about herself. The following is the content of that letter.

"About Me"

I was born 3rd March 1976. I had a family of 3 and myself making it 4 people. My Mum and Dad and my sister (elder) were killed in the civil war Liberia

I am a victim of power hungry maniacs. I lost everything and I have no hopes of a better future. I say so because of several reasons. One of which is, I escape from Liberia on the 28th October 1994 and arrived in German (Hamburg Harbour) by ship on the 28th December 1994.

I asked for a political asylum with the federal German office. I was sent to the former DDR (East Germany) for interview on the 4th January 1995. After this interviews I was posted to an asylum camp in Wismar.

I have spent a year in this camp without any decision from the authorities. I live here with fear, stress, frustration, depression and a state of confusion.

I am not allowed to work, go to school, or leave this town beyond 30 KM without a written permission from the branch of the federal bureau for refugees. In short we (refugees) are prisoners.

* * * * * * * *

Well, Mike, I guess there is more than one way to be imprisoned. This reached my heart because this individual is not guilty of any crime or action other than wanting to escape the oppression that killed her family members. For the most part we (BYU Independent Study Department) receive letters from students thanking us for the opportunity to continue their education. When one like this comes it brings us up short and we are washed over with gratitude for our blessings, and shame for our demanding attitudes, and resolve to be better people.

* * * * * * * *

Another form of imprisonment is sin. This past week, as part of my High Council duties, I sat in on a disciplinary council. A young man confessed to being involved in every imaginable form of sexual perversion. He is a returned missionary and is still struggling to overcome his habits. After a four hour session the President felt inspired to give the young man a clean slate to start with. He was excommunicated. My own feeling (sadly) is that the young man is still not resolved to give up some of his favorite sins. We shall see.

* * * * * * * *

By the way, can I come visit if I'm ever in that part of the state?

Dwight

Tune My Heart

"They say that they'd rather spend the rest of their life here, in prison, than return to Cuba! Some have committed crimes here in the joint just to assure they wouldn't get sent back."

March 17, 1996

Dear Dwight:

Here is my assignment. [As a typical professor I assigned Mike to write an essay on the song "Come Thou Fount of Every Blessing].

"Come, thou Fount of every blessing."

Let the blessings flow forth, from the original source. Like a stream flowing from the spring. C'mon with it! I'm ready to receive!

"Tune my heart to sing they grace."

Sing from the heart. (Not just words,) To sing about God's unmerited mercy towards mankind.

"Streams of mercy, never ceasing. . ."

The spring is everlasting. The mercy will continue to flow, and this is what calls for the "songs of loudest praise." Maybe the Lord likes some recognition. Some thanks every now and then.

"Teach me some melodious sonnet, sung by flaming tongues above."

Teach me something harmonious, sweet, and pleasing, as sung by the angels above.

"Praise the mount:"

Extol, worship, glorify the mountain; I picture the Sierras. Strong, solid.

"I'm fixed upon it."

Focused. Upon the

"Mount of thy redeeming love."

A mountain of love to free us from sin and it's consequences.

"O to grace how great a debtor daily I'm constrained to be!"

I'm forever in debt for the grace He has given me.

"Let Thy goodness, as a fetter, Bind my wandering heart to thee."

Self-explanatory. Chain my heart to thee. Please don't let it wander.

"Prone to wander, Lord, I feel it, Prone to leave the God I love."

Satan's temptations no doubt. Always tugging at the heart. You'll notice, in dealing with the Devil, that he'll often begin with a tiny little bargain just the smallest compromise. It will seem silly to object - after all, what he's offering is so great in comparison!

"Here's my heart, O take and seal it: seal it for thy courts above."

Take my heart Lord. Protect it from evil. I need to look good on judgement day! The problem, of course, is once you have compromised your principles in dealing with the Sulfuric One, your principles are compromised. The next compromise will be greater, and the next unbearable.

Well. . .how did I do for the first rough draft?

* * * * * * *

Now let's see. . .where were we? The story about Billie Bonta, the girl from Liberia, is <u>extremely</u> touching. I am enclosing a book of stamps. I know it's not much, but it's all I can come up with at this very moment. Air mail is expensive, I know. But if it will get one, maybe two lessons through, then I'll feel as though I have accomplished something.

I know you'll figure out a way to benefit her by it. <u>Please</u> accept them. I'm bending the rules here a little. But I'm willing to risk a little disciplinary action for a just cause.

* * * * * * *

Come to think of it, we do have a class of refugees here. Cuban exiles. The prison is full of them.

* * * * * * *

Now "Yak", he doesn't bother anybody. He just talks to himself and his seagull all day. Yes. He has a pet seagull in his cell. It must've come in a little low one day, perhaps in the fog, and got tangled up in the razor wire. Anyway, he's nursing it back to health. But the problem is, seagulls <u>never</u> get full. All they do is eat. And, well. . .when you constantly eat. . .you know what I mean. His cell is a total stinking mess! Literally speaking. But they do take showers. Together! I kid you not! They walk down the tier together. They even walk the same! It's comical.

* * * * * * *

Visiting? I can have the forms, i.e. questionnaire sent to you. Basically is what they do is a background check.

Sincerely,
<u>Mike</u>

We Must Wait Upon Him

"Let me know the cause of my stress on this beautiful morning."

April 16, 1996

Dear Mike:

I was thrilled with your treatise of "Come Thou Fount of Every Blessing". I give it an "A".

* * * * * * * *

Imagine preferring prison in America to returning to Cuba. Unbelievable!

* * * * * * * *

Please send me the visitation questionnaire (form). Who knows, maybe on some long, warm weekend I might just get the urge to jump on my motorcycle and ride southwest.

* * * * * * * *

Three weeks ago I awoke at 3am on a Sunday morning and couldn't get back to sleep. This was a strange thing for me because I never have trouble sleeping. I finally got up and told Linda I was going out for a walk. This really disturbed her because it hasn't happened in our 34 years of marriage. I walked around in the crisp cool air and listened to the birds and other sounds of spring. I looked to the east and the lights of the Provo temple beckoned so I walked over that direction and found myself walking around the temple. At a certain point I leaned against the wall of the temple grounds (which is locked at night) and had a serious and heartfelt talk with Heavenly Father. I asked if my life was acceptable. Many other questions and thoughts raced through my mind and I talked about them. How was I doing with my family? Would He forgive me of my sins? Why I hadn't been called to serve in any leadership positions in the church (an unrighteous questions)? Did I need more refining? Etc. Etc. Finally, I told Heavenly Father that I would strive to do whatever he wanted, however small or insignificant. Would he please put my mind at ease? As the eastern sky started to lighten I returned to a very worried wife (I had been gone 2 ½ hours. We sat and talked for another two hours. I told her I didn't know the cause of my stress but I had committed myself to be accepting of whatever the Lord wanted of me (even if I was called to be scoutmaster. . .joke!). We both showered and had breakfast and prepared for our Sunday School assignments. A knock came at the door and I opened it to find the entire Stake Presidency standing there. They came in and were very businesslike. They quickly informed me that they had come to release me from my calling as a High Councilor. I sat stunned and numb as they then proceeded to tell me I was called to be the Bishop of the BYU 76th ward. I couldn't respond, except to shake my head in the affirmative. The president made a few more remarks, then we had a kneeling prayer and they left.

* * * * * * * *

I look forward to your next letter. They are always so interesting, thought provoking, and enjoyable.

Dwight

Food Fight

"You would not believe the education I am getting in human behavior and abnormal psychology."

May 29, 1996

Dear Dwight:

I spotted a buzzard in the razor wire atop one of the fences, diligently pursuing a tasty morsel of some kind. From here it's hard to tell what it was. He's not very agile, but persistent. He succeeded in removing it from the wire and is tearing it to shreds right now. A crow is hip-hopping around behind the buzzard, making a lot of noise but unable to distract the larger bird. In fact, he appears a little annoyed with all the ruckus, and went after the crow.

Now, along comes one of the wild cats that scavenge the prison. He's stalking the buzzard. The buzzard pays little mind until the cat is in range. There's a brief stand-off. The buzzard makes the first move. Chases the cat off! Unbelievable! Whatever it is, it must be good. Now there are two cats fighting over it and the buzzard does not look too happy about it.

I know it could <u>not</u> have come out of the chow hall. Because I know not even a buzzard could stomach that!

* * * * * * * *

Thank you for the feedback on. . ."Fount of every Blessing."

* * * * * * * *

Your "premonition" is extremely inspiring. That's some pretty heavy intuition. Congratulations on your . . .promotion." That's not quite the word I'm seeking though, is it? But you know what I mean.

You knew <u>something</u> was coming, but you weren't quite sure what. Thank the good Lord above that it was <u>good</u>. That feeling of "not-knowing" is stressful. When I get that feeling I go to the beach, at night, alone.

There's something majestic in those powerful waves ruthlessly pounding the beach that really soothes my soul. I do miss it and look forward to it again.

Thank you for sharing that enlightening story with me. The sunrise and the songbirds too.

* * * * * * *

I'm starting to focus a little more on my priorities. Getting out of here right now is number one. That should happen in April, 2001. Right around the corner.

* * * * * * *

I will be "applying" for visiting forms to be sent to you. I would consider it an honor to meet you in person.

Sincerely,
Mike

Jury Duty

"The most critical aspect of a trial is the jury selection. They haggle over this long and hard because the case is often won or lost with the selection of the jury."

June 12, 1996

Dear Mike:

This bishop assignment has totally consumed my time--and I love it.

* * * * * * * *

Linda and I went to an opera where my friend performed the lead in Rigoletto. As we rose to leave Linda notice a diamond bracelet on the floor. I picked it up and walked over to the lady who had been sitting next to me. Without showing it to her I simply said, "Have you lost a bracelet"? She looked at her arm and then went a gray color and almost fainted. I reached out and handed her the bracelet. In a state of shock this sophisticated lady simply exclaimed "Oh (expletive-deleted)! Then she fell all over me thanking me for my honesty and she couldn't believe that I returned it. It had about 30 one carat diamonds, somewhere in the value range of $30-50,000. Linda and I went outside and laughed at how this prim and proper lady had lost her cool and let slip out the perfect word to express her feelings. We also thought it interesting that she was so amazed we had returned it. Of course it had never entered our minds to do anything else.

* * * * * * * *

We put about 2,000 miles on the motorcycles. We went from El Paso all the way down the west side of the state to Brownsville and finally out to South Padre Island in the Gulf of Mexico. The weather was perfect. Some highlights were Judge Roy Bean museum in Langtry, San Antonio river walk, the Alamo, Fredericksburg (a wild west decor of the street fronts) where Lyman Wight tried to settle a group of early Mormon colonists, the

Big Bend state park, longhorn cattle, a dog that run in front of me on the highway (I was doing about 70), and the biggest highlight of all was visiting the world's largest Harley-Davidson motorcycle shop in El Paso. We looked but we didn't buy -- couldn't afford them.

* * * * * * * *

Last week I was summoned for jury duty. Twenty-five people were there and the judge and attorney took about four hours to question us and decide on the final eight who would serve as the jury. It was a fascinating process. I was the only one there with a graduate degree. I saw one of the attorneys cross my name off the list the minute he heard me say I had a Ph.D. It would be intriguing to know why that would be such a turn-off for an attorney. I was dismissed.

* * * * * * * *

A lawyer friend told me that . . . the attorney's want a group of "common" citizens (whatever that means) that they can persuade and manipulate.

* * * * * * * *

I was thoroughly entertained by your description of the vulture and cat. Most of us are so busy that we don't see the little vignettes of drama that are probably all around us every day.

* * * * * * * *

Until next time.

Dwight

I'll Never Forget

"Would you mind bleeding somewhere else? I'm trying to eat here!"

July 28, 1996

Dear Dwight:

A lot of good things have started happening since we began this correspondence. I think attitude has a lot to do with it. My outlook on life has changed for the better. I'm feeling so good right now, I can hardly stand it! <u>Finally</u>, I am starting to see the light at the end of the tunnel.

It started out something like this: Last month I went to "Team". It's a three member panel that decides our fate. I was prepared. I had a letter of recommendation from my previous boss at work. Spoke highly of me. I was impressed! Because in here, behind these walls, there is rarely a kind word ever spoken.

I had transcripts of the college courses I have completed while incarcerated. Fourteen total, with a GPA of 3.72. Nothing spectacular in your world. But in here it's considered quite an accomplishment to some.

Fortunately for me, I was speaking to one of those people that appreciate and recognize someone who's trying to help himself. Especially when I mentioned BYU He was interested, because that is what captured his attention.

And now he was listening. That's when I mentioned Tucson, Arizona, and the Wastewater Treatment Program. [Mike was trying to get transferred from the penitentiary in Lompoc to the midway facility at Tucson where he could take some training]

They put me in for it. I was ecstatic to say the least! I could hardly contain my joy!

* * * * * * * *

The transfer, (I'm thinking positive) should be in August. Let's keep our fingers crossed. Nothing at this moment would make me happier, (except a full pardon of course) than getting out of this purgatory virtually unscathed.

31

* * * * * * * *

.It's been a ride, I'll say that. One I'll <u>never</u> forget.

For example, in the chow hall last week a guy gets his throat slashed at the dinner table. Not mine, thank God. But still. . .in the chow hall?

It looked like salsa all over everybody's beans and tortillas in the immediate vicinity. Please excuse me for being so graphic, but it really leaves an impression on the mind.

So what do you do in a situation like that? Eat fast. You're most likely getting locked down. And there's no telling when your next meal will arrive. No wonder I have indigestion!

* * * * * * * *

We have one of the World Trade Center bombers walking around here. [This was the bombing that was pre-9/11] He's actually worshiped by the rest of the militant Muslims. I just don't understand it. How can an all-caring, all-loving, all-powerful God let something or somebody like that do the things they do? How can He allow it to continue? How can He allow somebody to maliciously destroy the innocent and beautiful? (Which He has created.)

Those are just some of the questions that come to mind when something like this happens.

Then when I read about you and Linda at the opera house returning the bracelet, my faith in human nature once again is restored.

* * * * * * * *

Jury duty huh? That O.J. case was a fiasco here. A lot of people were stunned when he walked. It is truly amazing how easily a jury can be swayed by a fast talkin' attorney.

Myself, I took "the deal." "Door number 1, Door number 2, or Door number 3 Mr. Taylor. . .Which will it be?"

I had a fast-talkin' attorney who told me, "Sign right here on this dotted line or else you're lookin' at 25 years" (instead of 12). I couldn't sign fast enough! I told him, "Get those papers over here before they change their mind!"

* * * * * * * *

'Til the next time. . .   Take care.
Respectfully,
Mike

Old Friends

"Perhaps it will be best not to get reacquainted with all of them."

August 16, 1996

Dear Mike:

It was fun to read your letter. It had an air of excitement about it that hadn't surfaced in previous letters.

* * * * * * * *

It's graduation time around this campus and everyone is running around hugging each other and passing out congratulations. Perhaps that is the same euphoria you are experiencing with the possibility of a graduation to a different incarceration facility.

* * * * * * * *

Today I received a letter from a lady in Seattle, Washington. She expressed appreciation to Linda and me for sharing our son. He is on a mission there. She said, "Elder Laws has helped me with my teenage son (he's 14.) When I was telling Elder Laws how difficulty my son can be and how worried I was, he reassured me. He said he gave you plenty of hard times. But, he says later as he grew up he outgrew this phase and realized all you had done for him. I can't wait. I just wanted to reassure you your son is doing a terrific job on his mission. He's touching so many people and making a real difference." Of course I was very proud to receive such a letter. I thought of how much I loved him for his work and faithfulness.

* * * * * * * *

Yesterday as I was preparing to leave the temple after finishing a session, I was tying my tie while looking in the mirror and a guy in a black beard stood close behind me. I felt uncomfortable so I moved slightly to the side and continued to work on my tie. He moved over and put his head in close to mine. I thought, "What is this jerk doing?" He started to smile and I turned to say, I think you have mistaken me for someone else.

Before I could speak he said, "Hey fella, what the clang?" It really startled me because it has been almost 40 years since I had heard that expression. When I was a young teenager there were a bunch of us (6 or 8) who ran around together and that expression became our greeting (sort of like gangs today). When we picked up the phone and heard that expression we knew one of our group was calling. Anyway, it was Lowell (described as *Lovable* in my history I sent you a copy of). It was so much fun to see him again and we stood for a half hour and reminisced. What a blessing it is to have old friends and to be able to see them from time to time.

* * * * * * * *

I'm sure you will have some fun reunions with people in 4 ½ years. Perhaps it will be best not to get reacquainted with all of them (attempt at a joke). [Years later I would recall this statement with sadness.]

* * * * * * * *

Until next time.
Dwight

I Can See the Moon and Stars Again

"You would think that "the zookeepers" would be a little more appreciative of us. After all, "If it weren't for us. . .they'd be flipping burgers at McDonalds."

September 9, 1996

Dear Dwight:

Well. . .I almost made it to Tucson! The bus ride, 39 hours of pure misery is one more reason why I never want to return to prison!

They,"the big boys" in Washington said there is <u>no way</u> they'd let me go from a maximum security penitentiary directly to a low-security facility. I must do one year here first. Without any incidence reports, that is.

Hey. . .no problem! This place is like a country club. No stress. No tension. Just a big ol' health spa in the desert. Since you are a taxpayer, I'll spare you the details.

* * * * * * * *

I didn't know if I mentioned this previously or not. But since our correspondence began, some really positive things have started happening to me. Call it coincidence, call it what you may, but whatever it is, I'm liking it! My attitude and entire outlook on life has changed dramatically.

* * * * * * * *

Keep this under your hat because I don't want to shock my parents; but I have even considered attending church services again. They do offer LDS services here.

* * * * * * * *

Dwight, I am feeling so good again I can hardly stand it! I hope this isn't just another one of life's cycles. I know there'll always be "highs" and "lows", but this seems almost too good to be true. And I'm still locked up! That's what is so hard to believe. I like who I see in the mirror now.

* * * * * * * *

Onward: "What the clang. . ?" If anybody from here meets me on the street, you know what I'm doing??? Breaking <u>all</u> track records! Exit, stage left. . .I'm outta here!!! All this running I'm doing ain't for nuttin'! [Michael didn't know this statement has come back to haunt me – Dwight.]

* * * * * * *

You should be receiving your visitation forms soon. And as always, I anxiously await your next letter.

'Til then, take care and I hope that <u>all</u> is well. . .

Respectfully,
Mike

Here I come

"On my motorcycle."

October 13, 1996

Dear Mike:

Instead of sending my usual letter on the 16th of this month, I am coming to visit.

* * * * * * * *

Please send me back a quick note answering the following questions. You'll have to do it immediately or I won't get your answer before I leave.

1- How long can I visit? Can I have multiple visits?
2- Any instructions about dress?
3- Can I bring things such as books, food, clothes, radios, TV, computer, etc.? If so what would you like to have?
4- Can I give you money while I am there?
5- What other instructions do you have for me?

Dwight

Instructions

"<u>Please</u> drive carefully! I know you like to go fast"!

October 19, 1996

Dear Dwight:

Enclosed is the information you requested. [Mike sent a boiler plate instruction sheet that is given to all potential visitors.] I "hi-lited" what I felt was important. One important fact they left out: You can <u>not</u> wear khakis. They won't let you in if you are wearing anything that resembles my clothing.

* * * * * * *

We can visit for the duration of visitation hours: 4:30-8:00 P.M. (Mon. Tues., Fri.) Multiple visits are allowed. All you can bring is <u>you</u>. And picture I.D. <u>Very</u> important. <u>No</u> books, food etc.

They do have vending machines for our convenience. This is the only money you are allowed to bring inside the institution. No large bills.

* * * * * * *

See you on Friday!

Respectfully,
Mike

The Visit

". . a big smile and a vigorous handshake."

October 29, 1996

Dear Mike:

What an incredible experience it was to visit with you. I wrote my feelings in my journal and thought you might enjoy reading them. Here goes.

I just returned from my visit with Mike. My mind was on the visit for days before I went and I have pondered and processed the experience almost constantly since the visit. Mike is an incredible guy. I can't explain to myself why I have felt such a bond with him but I know the brief correspondence we have had and the short three hour visit have been very satisfying to my soul. The experience, as a total, has changed my life in small but significant ways. All of my life I have admired people who have courage. People who overcome great odds and difficulty and make something of themselves have always been my heroes.

For several days before the visit I was nervous as well as excited. The closest I can come to describing the feeling is to remember my first blind date. What would I say? What would I do? Would I make a fool of myself? How would we fill up the three hours? I needn't have worried. Mike was easy to know and to talk with. I was amazed when we were interrupted with the announcement that visiting hours were over. It was all too soon. I wish I could drop by several times a week for a chit-chat. But I am back home, 700 miles away, so I will be pleased to continue with the correspondence only. Maybe next year I can justify another motorcycle ride to Phoenix, or preferably to Tucson.

On the day of the visit I was so nervous and didn't want to miss the opportunity so I rode the 26 miles from my hotel to the facility just to time the trip. I ended up at the first building and went in to check out the lobby.

I was informed I had arrived at the women's facility. So I rode on up the road and checked out the location of the men's facility. I then rode back to Bell Road where I found a cinema complex and I went in and watched movies until time to drive back to the prison. I arrived at 4:25 and went in. I was totally ignored by the man working the counter. I was going to speak up but I was so intrigued I decided I was going to make this a little experiment (always the researcher). I made myself a promise I would make a friend out of this man. I knew it is hard to make friends with someone who doesn't respect you. I also assumed that intimidation and power are factors in this type of a facility. Therefore, I quickly made up my mind to control the situation. I stood by the desk and didn't utter a word. I waited for what seemed like five minutes and I could feel the tension building but I simply waited. Finally, his comfort level and feeling of superiority was shaken enough he finally muttered, "What can I do for you?"

I explained that I thought I had been approved for visitation rights. He asked for my papers and I told him I didn't have any. That immediately put him back in charge and he informed me he didn't have any authorization. I played to his need to be in charge by assuring him I was confident he knew how to get that authorization. This tweaked his pride a little so he responded by asking who I was visiting.

"Michael Taylor"

"We have many Michael Taylors" (sarcastically and triumphantly and also a lie - they only had two))

"Michael J. Taylor" (I screwed this up. It's Michael S. Taylor)

"We don't have any Michael J. Taylors" (another victory for him) "What unit is he in?"

I didn't know of course but I happened to glance at the directory on the wall and so I took a chance.

"I think he is in the Navajo Unit" (first one I noticed on the directory)

"We don't have a Michael Taylor in the Navajo Unit." (another victory for him)

"Maybe it was the Yuma unit, I'm not sure." (second one I saw on the directory)

I thought I had a victory here because he looked at his computer screen and said,

"Just a minute" (long pause while he looks at screen) "The Michael Taylor in this unit is not cleared for any visitors." (another victory for him)

At this point I wanted to pick up the little pipsqueak by the jacket collar and ring his evil little neck. Then I remembered my promise to myself to make a friend out of him. "I've come 700 miles to visit Michael. I was told this had been pre-approved. It looks like the only way its going to work for me is if you can solve this for me." He looked at me with the look of the victor and said, "please sit over there and wait." I walked over to where he had pointed, but I didn't sit down. I showed a small measure of defiance by standing. Actually, I had been sitting on the motorcycle for two days and really didn't mind standing for a few minutes. After about ten minutes my adversary looked up and said, "by the way visiting hours don't start until 5pm anyway". I could see there was no use in pointing out to him that Chapter II of the visiting regulations, which the prison published, clearly reads, "Visiting hours are . . .Fridays from 4:30 p.m. (Or after the 4:00 p.m. count clears) until 8:30 p.m."

Ten minutes later he looked up again. "You a relative of Michael Taylor?" "No." "Long time friend?" "No." "Have you ever visited him before?" "No." "Have you ever met him before?" "No."

At this point it was becoming comical to me. I hope I didn't give my feelings away with a hint of a smile. The whole thing was starting to sound ridiculous and I could see the seeds of doubt quickly crossing his face. The inevitable question finally came. "Then why did you want to visit him?" In the most desperate way I wanted to say "None of your business." But reason prevailed and I explained we had a long correspondence going and this was the first opportunity we had to finally meet. He still didn't seem convinced so he dropped his head and ignored me for another five minutes.

After he had made me wait a respectful amount of time to show who was in charge he finally raised his head and said, "Richard, you have been cleared. I found Michael in the Mohave Unit." Of course he knew that all along because there were only two Michael Taylors, but he strung me out as long as possible. I'm sure he felt like he had the final victory in our little struggle of wills. I showed the proper amount of appreciation by telling him I was grateful he worked so hard to solve my problem. His reaction made me wonder if he had ever been complimented in his miserable life.

I followed up with an attempt at chit-chat by asking him what I could and could not take into the facility with me (I already knew because Michael had already briefed me). He was more than happy to spout out regulations and rules. He instructed me to put everything else in a locker, which I did. Finally, at approximately 5:30 a security guard came and announced he was here to take us into the visiting area.

But it was not over. Another episode of authoritative behavior was yet to be endured. I learned that we would go through three double locked security stations. We would enter one door and then it would lock behind us before the exit door would open. As we approached the first entrance door to the first lock station we found an officer that had taken the control panel off the security lock and was fiddling with it. He mentioned it needed repair. We all stood and waited another 15 minutes while he played with the lock. He could have very easily let us enter the room during the many times that he manually opened the door, but he wouldn't do it. We weren't allowed to budge until he had repaired the door. Then he deliberately tested it about four times before he finally let us pass. Even the security guard who was our guide was visibly upset at this display. When the door was finally opened for our entrance the repairman stood and glared at each of us as we passed. I don't know if we were supposed to be impressed with him and his badge or if he expected us to be afraid of him. I was neither. In fact I was really starting to enjoy myself as I watched and learned about this mini-culture out in the desert. The thought that came to my mind was, "well these people are certainly not concerned about customer relations."

As I exited the third lockout room I heard my name and looked up to see, on the other side of some bars, Mike smiling at me. I recognized him because he had sent pictures in one of his letters. I waved and then was ushered into the visiting room. We sat in there for another fifteen minutes until the inmates were allowed in. Mike walked in and came over with a big smile and gave me a vigorous handshake. He is about 6' 2" tall, dark wavy hair, with a small gray streak that made him look very distinguished. He wears a Tom Selleck mustache (which I both admired and envied), and he is extremely fit. He works on the weights, watches his diet, and has made himself into an excellent physical specimen. In short he is an extremely handsome and imposing figure. I remembered back to when I had shown his picture to some of the women in my office. They all fell in love with him immediately.

He has dark eyes that hint of a strange combination of past hurt, submerged anger, wariness, intelligence and a large dose of mischief. He is very observant, probably a survival skill he has learned. He measures carefully all he looks at and his eyes dart around giving one the impression he doesn't miss a thing. I got the impression that he is probably a master of reading body language and environmental communications of all sorts. On the other hand his eyes and expression are warm and friendly and he possesses a wonderfully bright and inviting smile. I immediately felt comfortable and it was as though I was visiting an old buddy I had known for a lifetime. Though we had just met I think it might be we will be friends from this time forward.

Our conversation was a pleasant and even exciting exchange. I can't remember everything that was said but there were some poignant moments for me and a few things I will note here. He has rubbed shoulders with serial murderers and bombing terrorists. He has observed multiple incidents of man's inhumanity to man. He has learned to avoid potentially deadly situations. He has lived in a community of complex caste systems. He has learned to anticipate the actions of cliques, gangs and crazy inmates. He knows how to keep his mouth shut and what to say when he opens it. Mike explained to me how he reads the attitude of others by how they walk, their pace, how they swing their shoulders, where they focus their eyes and how to respond to all of these messages.

In addition Michael has learned other survival skills such as learning to regiment his routines to avoid the madness of solitude. He has discovered reading, weight lifting, running, and other activities help him avoid the mind numbing hours of TV, card playing, or walking through the dim and foggy half-existence of a drug induced semi-comma. He has somehow sorted out attributes people have and knows that happiness is better than hate and bitterness. He knows there is hope, in spite of being surrounded by despair. He has grown past the human failing of blaming all of his misfortune on someone or something else. He has learned responsibility and he has the courage to accept it. To me he is simply amazing. I sincerely doubt I could have walked in his moccasins and not completely drown in it all.

We had some fun exchange and some laughter. He told me his cellies wanted to know why a director of a major department at a major university would travel 700 miles to see him when I was not a relative and had never met him before. They probably still wonder just what is going on. They probably don't believe him any more than the guard believed my explanation. Perhaps it isn't so hard to understand their disbelief. When I returned home and reported what I had been doing, there were several people in my own office that wanted to know why I would go so far to visit someone I had never known or met.

Mike shared with me some of his life, his joys and sorrows. He has a daughter and a son. He has a childhood sweetheart that is still probably his best friend. Although she is married she still loves him and is doing a good job of raising the son they had together. Mike loves his parents and siblings. He is well read and speaks and corresponds at a level consistent with what one would expect from a college graduate.

During our conversation I observed other visitors and inmates. Probably a large majority were minorities. It seemed most visitors were wives. One sad situation was an old farmer and his wife visiting a son. I can imagine the son wanted to get away from the farm and went about it the wrong way. One couple stood holding each other for the entire three hours, whispering and swaying in a sort of a dance. Others seemed to smile, give each other a kiss and then quickly lapse into serious discussions or even arguments.

I was really pleased to discover Mike had made arrangements for one of the personnel to come and take our picture together. The man came in and had us stand for a couple of snap shots. It will be really fun to get copies of those pictures. Mike promised to send them along when he gets them.

Mike and I had a short conversation about the guards. Probably most of them have a minimal education, work all day, go home to trailer parks to grouchy wives and howling kids and then come back the next day to spend it in the same place as Mike. We laughed and raised the rhetorical question of "who was really in prison here".

Mike has a very concrete and admiral goal to qualify for a transfer to the Tucson facility and be a candidate for wastewater treatment training. He wants to be prepared for his release. I hope it works and that I get another opportunity to go visit him in Tucson.

All too soon the announcement came that visiting hours were over. I stood and shook Mikes hand and then gave him an embrace. Wow! The guy is made of steel. I wouldn't want him for an enemy. Fortunately, I consider him a wonderful friend. As I left the visitors area I turned for another wave and smile at Mike. It felt strangely like I had on several occasions when I saw my sons leave for missions. The final wave really gives a tug at the heart.

We worked our way back through the same double lock system until we were again in the entrance foyer. I purposely waited to be last to leave the entrance area. I stayed behind to have a final conversation with my antagonist. When the opportunity presented itself I said, "I really appreciate all the work you did to see I was able to make this visit. You had to jump through hoops and go the extra mile to help me didn't you?" He smiled for the first time and said, "Well I try to do what I can to help people when they come here" (yeah, right!) I praised him some more and his smile broadened and I left with a friendly wave and yet another expression of appreciation. He never realized I had the final victory -- I got him to smile and to be my friend.

End of journal entry. Thanks for your wonderful hospitality. You treated me like a trusted family member and that was very important to me. I fought a strong headwind for 230 miles on my ride back to St. George but arrived safely. More in December.

Dwight

Be Nice to Bruce

". . . you would never, never, never be-
lieve it. Not in a million years!

But after he did it . . ."

November 23, 1996

Dear Dwight:

Did you really come see me. . .or, was it just a dream? I stopped and asked myself numerous times, "What have I done to deserve this great honor?"

"Why would a man in your position want to come 700 miles out of the way (and back again!) Just to see me?" This was question number two, racing through my mind.

I was nervous at first. But immediately upon walking into the visiting room, I was overcome with a calmness that set me completely at ease. It was like we have known each other for. . .well. . .forever! It was like we were two ol' drinkin' buddies bellied up to the bar. Ooops! <u>Bad</u> analogy! Just kidding!!!

Seriously though, I talked more in those three short hours than I have in the last three years! It's highly unusual for me just opening up like that. I felt as though I had nothing to hide. I was <u>totally</u> relaxed.

The next morning, I went out and ran, just like I said. But this run was unique. My feet weren't even touching the ground! I was floating. . .no. . .I was flying!

Sure enough, when I looked to the west, there it was, imminent, impending and threatening. A huge storm looming on the horizon. Then I heard thunder. . .or was it Dwight? On his motorcycle. . .with less than a dime on the road. . .breaking a new land speed record!

I leaned into the wind, and ran a little faster. "Let the thunder roll. . ." I was feeling pretty good. And this day, you brought the best out in me.

And that little hug at the end. . .I felt as thought I was touched by an angel of God. . .

* * * * * * *

I really enjoyed your journal entry about our visit.

* * * * * * *

Dwight & Mike

* * * * * * *

Out there, in the real world, the guards are nobody. And then, like you said, they put on that uniform and suddenly they're Superman! Of course, there are <u>always</u> exceptions. But generally speaking, most of 'em walk around in their 'inflated' state of superiority.

Here's a first-rate example: (And a good reason I wished I kept a journal while at United Sates Penitentiary, Lompoc.)

I was taken downtown one day to see the eye doctor. Two guards snatched me right of the "iron-pile" (weight-pile). Told me not to say a word to nobody. At first I thought I was going to 'the hole." But breathed a sigh of relief when we passed SH-unit" and went downstairs to R&D (Receiving & Distribution). The penitentiaries bus depot. There I was dressed in the proper attire, to make sure I didn't have anything concealed in my clothing. While changing, they made sure you don't have anything concealed anywhere else either.

When I was "dressed out," I was adorned with more chain then I would care to swim with. An added extra attraction is a black-box snapped over the handcuffs, padlocked shut, which is all chained to a chain that wraps around your waist, and between the legs. Don't forget the leg irons either. And the piece of paper you now must sign stating you understand "deadly force" may be used against you. Houdini himself could not have designed a better implement of torture. The sad part is, it was a convict who designed the apparatus! I know at least one person who'd love to catch him walking the line someday! Of course, you know I'm just kidding. . .(yeah right!!)

Now it's time for them to suit up. Bullet-proof vests? Check. Side-arms? Check. Shotguns? Check. M-16? Check. . .Check. . .Check. And last but not least, THE SPEECH.

This is where they all gather around, kind of close and lean on you a little bit. And whisper, real low, inexplicable words and threats not even worth printing. I guess this was supposed to be some kind of intimidation factor. (See me shaking?) They yank on the chains too, just for emphasis.

Hey, all I want is to see a real doctor. Not one of these foreign quacks imported from who-knows-where!

They gave John, my co-worker, some eye-drops one day for a similar problem. When he returned to his cell, bottle in hand, something told him to read the label first. There it was, in plain English: "Do not put in eyes. May cause blindness!" Was he furious? Boy-Howdeee!

"So you'll have no problem outta me boys. . ." Let's roll. They load me into an armored car. A brinks armored car! It looked like they were transporting a billion dollars of gold bullion. They even had a chase-car following.

When we step out at the doctors office, it looked like some kind of military drill. One covered the rooftops, one covered the parking lot. Two covered me, while two stormed the offices to make sure nobody was lying in wait.

The prisoner was brought in. No waiting. I received immediate attention.

When the doctor asked me, "Why are you smiling?", I wanted to tell him, "Who do you think they'll shoot first, me or you?" The guy who had the gun on me was more nervous than a long-tailed cat in a room full of rocking chairs! I'm surprised he didn't shoot himself in the foot! That would have triggered the fusillade! Everybody in the doctor office would've been dead before the smoke cleared!

These were the thoughts running through my mind as I couldn't help but overhear "the tyrants" bragging how tough they were.

That poor little secretary couldn't even get her work done. It's the "balloon theory" Dwight. They had it bad this day! She was cute too. This just added fuel to the fire. Boy...were they pumping themselves up!

They were telling her "war stories" from "The Pen." How they smash our heads into the concrete, etc...etc...etc...Everything they were saying was true. What they neglected to tell her is when they do come like that, it's thirty-to-one, their favor!

So I'm just sitting there, smiling to myself, listening to all this gibberish of how tough they are. Well, if they're sooo tough, (and the secretary, she kept smiling at me), if they're soo tough; then I must be one Baaad Dude!

* * * * * * *

They just love stereotyping us. This way, later on, suppose something happens. Let's say, I walk into the post office and kill all my co-workers. They can say, "yep...We knew it. See here? The handwriting was on the wall. He fits the profile!" That's their favorite phrase.

The reason I use the post office analogy is because of Bruce. Lil' Ol' Bruce. The kindest, sweetest little old man you'll ever meet. Killed his dog, then his mother (because he knew he wouldn't be able to take care of them anymore). Reloads, goes to the post-office and kills seven or nine co-workers. Finds one hiding in the closet. And tells him or her, "You can go. You've always been nice to me. . ." Wow!!!

What's the moral of the story? Be nice to Bruce! But looking at the guy you would never, never, never believe it. Not in a million years! But after he did it, the Feds step in and say, "yep. . .we knew it all along. Because he fits-the-profile."

* * * * * * *

Okay. How about we depart on a little lighter note? Some humor perhaps? Well, this electrician was doing something in a guys cell. So he sets up a step and proceeds to climb up it, and stuck his head right in the ceiling fan which was <u>humming</u>!

They sound like a helicopter taking off when you turn'em up! Anyway, it parts his hair in about seven new directions (thump! thump! thump!) Breaks his nose and blackens both eyes! Ever been beat up by a ceiling fan? I don't recommend it.

Knocks him clear off the ladder and he hits his head on a locker on the way down, where they find him flopping around like a fish. (Doin' "the tuna" is the term.)

The guard is summoned. He panics. Hits the "panic button". They <u>all</u> panic. <u>Everybody</u> comes running. It's really something to see. Staff responding to a "body alarm". It reminds me of the "Keystone Cops."

One cop lost his shoe. Somebody hid it. He was mad! Walked around the rest of the day with one shoe, looking for the other one! We all paid dearly for that.

They didn't believe anybody was stupid enough to stick his whole head in a ceiling fan and thought somebody "piped" him.

Boy, I'll tell you what. It doesn't take much to entertain us, does it!

* * * * * * * *

Thanx again Dwight for the <u>wonderful</u> visit. Til the next time, with the most profound respect.

<u>Mike</u>

Going the Extra Mile

"seeking out the lost sheep' has a very special mean-
ing when the sheep is my own."—Gerald Taylor

December 16, 1996

Dear Dwight:

During our visit with Michael on Thanksgiving Day he informed us, in detail, of your visit to him. I can't adequately express my appreciation to you for the interest you have shown for Michael and for your extraordinary kindness to visit with him.

* * * * * * *

With warm regards
Gerald Taylor (Mike's father)

Merry Christmas

"The bottom line is that all of us (I mean every living soul) is a child of God."

December 16, 1996

Dear Mike:

I loved your last letter. My assistant director walked passed my office and said, "Dwight what are you laughing about, I could hear you out here?" I had just finished the episode of the guy that was mugged by the overhead fan. Great story. Of course I felt compassion for this poor unfortunate man, but your description of the events was so well written I hee-hawed through it all. Since the man survived I hope I am not too wicked for having a good laugh over "parted hair," "Keystone Cops," and "doin the tuna."

Actually, I was already in a jovial mood when I got to that part because I was enjoying your story about the visit to the eye doctor. I understand why they do such things, but nevertheless your narrative was most enjoyable. Have you ever thought of becoming a stand-up comic?

* * * * * * *

Your little treatise on "stereotyping" was also very well written. I chuckled at your moral. . .in fact I think I will use your moral as another guideline for my life. BE NICE TO BRUCE. Good advice in any situation. There is much irony in the concept of being able to see the obvious, *after the fact.* I now have an excellent option for the conclusion of our correspondence in five years. If you screw up and don't get released or have more time added (heaven forbid) then I can say, "I knew it all along. He thought he was going to get out but I could tell he wasn't the right type. I could tell he was a bad seed and something would happen and he would mess up again. I knew it all along. He fits the stereotype." On the other hand, when you get out (notice my positive statement here) I can say, "I told you so. I knew a good man when I saw one. I am a wonderful judge of character. He was made of the right stuff. He fit perfectly the profile of a reformed man. I told you so. I had no doubt whatsoever." The whole thing is really nonsense isn't it? The bottom line is all of us (I mean every living soul) is a child of God. We all have merit, value and worth. We all have potential. We all make mistakes. We all have achievements. The only valid profile or stereotype is our eternal genealogy.

* * * * * * * *

I mailed a box of printed matter to you for Christmas. I hope they let you have it. There was a set of church history books, a Far Side calendar, and a paper back Book of Mormon. Since nothing is hardback I hope it is allowed through. The Book of Mormon is probably just a duplicate for you, the Far Side is something I'm sure you will enjoy, but the history library may not appeal to you too much. I guess since I found it so fascinating to read I thought you might enjoy some of it. It read it about ten years ago, every word, and it took me about six month to wade through it. At least it may be a good reference source for you. I certainly won't be offended if you find it is as exciting as reading the dictionary.

* * * * * * * *

Mike, I want to take this opportunity to wish you a Merry Christmas and a Happy New Year. Under your circumstances that may be a misplaced wish, but on the other hand you most of all would understand.

Christ spoke of those who professed to be righteous but omitted the weightier matters of the law. He said, "I was a stranger, and ye took me not in: naked, and ye clothed me not: sick, and in prison, and ye visited me not." What an indictment! What a sad commentary. I hope that you and I are not guilty of this offense.

But there is a brighter, glorious scenario. Christ speaking to the humble saints said, (Matt 25:34-39) Then shall the King (Christ) say unto them on his right hand, Come, ye blessed of my Father, inherit the kingdom prepared for you from the foundation of the world: For I was an hungred, and ye gave me meat: I was thirsty, and ye gave me drink: I was a stranger, and ye took me in: Naked, and ye clothed me: I was sick, and ye visited me: I was in prison, and ye came unto me. Then shall the righteous answer him, saying, Lord, when saw we thee an hungred, and fed thee? Or thirsty, and gave thee drink? When saw we thee a stranger, and took thee in? Or naked, and clothed thee? Or when saw we thee sick, or in prison, and came unto thee? And the King shall answer and say unto them, Verily I say unto you, *Inasmuch as ye have done it unto one of the least of these my brethren, ye have done it unto me."* I pray that we (you and I, and our loved ones) will be among this chosen group who are invited to set on his right hand.

May you have the spirit fill your bosom to the bursting point. May you feel the warmness of the Spirit at this time of the year. Even though you are in prison it is my wish for you that you will have at least one moment where you feel so good you want to jump up and shout. May you have at least one other moment where you drop to your knees in humility and gratitude for all the Lord has blessed you with. I will be thinking of you through this wonderful season. I will pray for your welfare, well-being, and contentment. I will pray for us both to have PEACE.

God bless you, Mike!

Dwight

John Taylor

"I am a direct descendant."

February 6, 1997

Dear Dwight:

As you can see, I'm running a little behind. Thank you for being so patient.

And thanx to you, I am now a proud owner of "The History of the Church. Also, I received the Book of Mormon, your letter, the money and "The Far Side" calendar to keep me laughing <u>all</u> year long!

* * * * * * * *

I started with the "History of the Church." Of course I couldn't resist. I went directly to the section on John Taylor, whom I am a direct descendant thereof. A fascinating man and a fascinating story (vol. 7) about the lynch mob and how he survived.

I vaguely remember my father telling me that story. I was in a museum in Salt Lake City I believe. The pocket watch was encased in glass. The watch that saved my great, great… grandfather's life.

* * * * * * * *

All is well here.

Respectfully
<u>Mike</u>

A Humor Break

"Is there another word for synonym?"

February 20, 1997

Dear Mike:

I fussed and fretted and worried. Your letter didn't come so I checked to see if I had missed on the calendar and if it was actually my turn to write. It was your turn so I instructed my associate to FAX your letter if it came while I was away in Washington D.C. It did. . .and he did.

* * * * * * * *

Here are a few "deep thought" questions that may add a little humor to your day. If you have the answer to any of them I would appreciate your response. Maybe you can have fun by asking them, in a most serious manner, to "Big Money". [Big Money is a loud mouth know-it-all who is incarcerated with Mike] Who knows maybe he will give you answers that will amuse you even more than the questions. Here goes. . .

- If a mute swears, does his mother wash his hands with soap?
- Is there another word for synonym?
- Why do they lock gas station bathrooms? Are they afraid someone will clean them?
- If a stealth bomber crashes in a forest, will it make a sound?
- If you're cross-eyed and have dyslexia, can you read all right
- Why do they sterilize the needles for lethal injections?
- How did a fool and his money get together?
- Why do kamikaze pilots wear helmets?
- What was the best thing before sliced bread? (My personal favorite)

Now, in case none of these questions stump "Big Money" then you might ask him if he knows what big companies pack Styrofoam in when they ship it.

* * * * * * *

I was pleased to see your delight at researching about John Taylor. We all love those stories but not many of us can call him grandpa. The next time you go to the museum and look at that watch I hope I am with you.

* * * * * * *

A few weeks ago my motorcycle buddy had to go to North Carolina to visit his daughter. I said, "Why don't you take my pickup and load the bikes on it and drive back"? He did. Then he came home. Our bikes are now in Raleigh N.C. About the 20th of March he is going to fly back there. I will drive my pickup to my cousins place north of Dallas and park it there and fly to Raleigh. We will then ride our bikes through North Carolina (including Kitty Hawk), South Carolina, Georgia, Florida, Alabama, Mississippi, Louisiana, and finally back to Dallas where we will load the bikes and haul them back home. I am really excited and pumped. My next letter will be full of biker stories (hopefully most of them will be true).

* * * * * * *

You are in my mind, and in my prayers, and I hope your spirit will remain high.

Dwight

P.S. I received a nice Christmas card from your folks with a letter enclosed. It was one of my special Christmas presents. You also should be proud of your parents. I was extremely touched by their words of love for you.

A Fool and His Money

"Don't rob a bank where you have an account."

March 15, 1997

Dear Dwight:

If a mute swears, does his mother wash his hands with soap? Yes! Dial soap. The same kind Mom used to wash my mouth out with! Yuck!!! She would rub it across our teeth this way, and that way. . .side to side, so little pieces would get stuck in between and I would have to taste it for hours! Boy. . . would I be swearing then! Under my breath of course.

* * * * * * * *

While we're still in the swearing mode, it brings to mind a rich Texas oilman and his son.

Well, his first son was perfect. Perfect in every way. This is why it was such a tragedy when he lost his beautiful son.

He was so devastated he decided he wanted another one. Identical. So he hired a team of scientists to clone him a new son. A clone of the wonderful boy he just lost.

As the years went on, he realized what a terrible mistake he had made. Sure, the boy looked the same, but the personalities were <u>totally</u> opposite. This kid was rotten! He couldn't take him anywhere for the simple fact that every other word that came out of the boy's mouth was obscene.

So the despairing father takes the boy to the top of an oil rig, and pushes him off. Of course the kid is screaming profanities all the way down.

Since the kid was a clone, the Texas jury was hung on whether or not the father actually committed murder. After hours of lengthy deliberations they finally reached a verdict: The father was guilty of making an obscene clone fall.

O.K.. .Enough already! But remember, you started it!

* * * * * * * *

How did a fool and his money get together? That's an easy one. Just walk into a bank, jump up on the counter and scream, "Everybody on the floor!!!" Just don't do it at the local bank where you have an account. Especially when there is a sheriff parked in the parking lot! True story. Except for the part of jumping up on the counter. They only do that in the movies.

* * * * * * *

Respectfully
Mike

Do I Dare Ask?

"How did you plan those robberies?"

April 16, 1997

Dear Mike:

"Making an obscene clone fall", indeed! Ok, Ok I started it. You are actually very clever in answering all of those inane questions and statements. I was pleased with your synonym for a synonym (clone...why didn't I think of that). And as for a "fool and his money" you gave the perfect answer. I laughed about it many times and told everyone who would listen.

* * * * * * * *

I just told my friend Roy here at the office about your jokes so he gave me this one to send back. "A beautiful young lady gets sick and tired of dizzy blond jokes so she has her hair dyed and a complete makeover. Even buys a new car to help change the image. She takes a drive to the country and comes upon a sheepherder. "I have a proposition for you", she says to the sheepherder. "If I can tell you exactly how many sheep you have can I have one?" "Sure, why not", he responds. She says "382". "Amazing", he says, "your exactly right. Help yourself to one of the sheep." She browses among the sheep and picks one and puts it in her car. "Now I have a proposition for you", the sheepherder says. "Go ahead", she responds. He asks, "If I can guess the true color of your hair can I have my dog back?" If you don't like it just remember it came from Roy, not me.

* * * * * * * *

You said jumping on the counter is only done in the movies and that triggered a question in my mind. Do I dare ask??? I think I will. You can always refuse to answer. How did you plan those robberies and what did you do. Do the movies depict any of it correctly? Did you have a particular style? Were there do's and don'ts that you functioned with? Were you the master mind? Am I getting to personal or offensive? Would answering such questions get you in trouble? If so, please ignore. If you are willing to answer my presumptuous questions then I will be bold enough to ask you to answer them in some detail. I'm totally intrigued. Like I said don't answer if you don't want to. Perhaps I have presumed too much upon our friendship to even ask you. If so, I apologize.

* * * * * * * *

Now for your tour of the South. As you know early in the spring my friend John had hauled our bikes to North Carolina and left them at his daughters place. On March 21ˢᵗ I drove to Dallas and left my pickup at the airport (had to stop in Trinidad, Colorado for a complete brake job, including turning the drums and disks). Then I flew to Raleigh, North Carolina via Houston, and met John at his daughters. We began our tour by riding over to the Atlantic coast and spending the first night. Early the next day we went to Kitty Hawk to see the place where the Wright Brothers made the first flight. It was very exciting for both of us because we are both pilots (John used to fly jets and he worked on the SR71, the sleek looking blackbird). Then we rode south down Cape Hatteras and took two different ferry boats to get us back to the mainland near the South Carolina border. That night it rained hard. The next morning it was still raining but by the time we finished breakfast it had stopped so we continued our ride through Myrtle Beach, South Carolina and spent the next night at Charleston, an old plantation and seaboard city of pre-revolutionary war fame. Charleston is also the site of the beginning of the Civil War (Fort Sumpter). Joseph Smith prophesied 30 years earlier the war would start in South Carolina.

The next day we rode to Savannah, Georgia. From Savannah we headed across Georgia. We stopped along the way for some fresh peach ice cream. We then stayed the next night at my daughter's near Montgomery, Alabama. That was really great to spend time with four of my grandchildren. The next day we stopped in the middle of the day at a air museum we stumbled across somewhere in Mississippi. We went in and John got excited when we discovered it was showcasing an SR71. John checked the numbers on it and sure enough it was the one he had been assigned to years earlier. Almost brought tears to his eyes. Our ride across Louisiana was uneventful and then we rode into Texas and back to Dallas.

* * * * * * * *

I have some exciting things happening here at home. My daughter who got divorced last October has found a law student who is also divorced and they have decided to get married. It will be a civil marriage and they have asked me to do it. As Bishop I can do that. I had to write to the First Presidency to get approval since neither one of them actually live in the ward I am bishop of. Also my last son is leaving on his mission in a few weeks. His farewell is being held this Sunday and I have to prepare a talk.

* * * * * * *

My son is going to Baltimore on his mission. He wanted to go to a foreign country and I kiddingly told him he got his wish.

* * * * * * *

Keep up the courage. I really do believe with all my heart that God loves us and cares for us (you and me) and that he will bless us. May it be so for you.

Dwight

Bank Robbery 101

*"What finally inspired me was the Colum-
bia School of Broadcasting."*

May 18, 1997

Dear Dwight:

As you can see it is Sunday afternoon and all is well. Life is great.

I am enjoying a few precious moments of solitude. My "celly" is on a visit, so this is a rare moment. Alone at last!

* * * * * * * *

Now, let's see if I can answer some of your questions.

Bank Robbery 101: (Please do not try this at home!)

My modus operandi was simple. However, it took time to build up the courage. What finally inspired me was the Columbia School of Broadcasting.

I was watching television one afternoon (first mistake.) The commercial comes on. This guy gives a magnificent speech about, "you'll never know until you try. . ." You must understand that I was already contemplating criminal activity. Ping! The light comes on. "You know something. . ." I tell myself, "He's right!"

I turned the television off, went to the garage and sawed off a 12 gauge, pump shotgun. <u>Totally</u> unnecessary. Total overkill. (No pun intended.) Total stupidity. I thank the good Lord above nobody was ever hurt.

Then I purchase some totally ridiculous clothes at the Goodwill. Too big. Way out of fashion. They were my throw-away clothes that went over the top of my regular clothes. Two complete sets in other words. And it was <u>HOT</u> that day!

My getaway vehicle was a bicycle that I parked in the bushes next to a church, next to the bank.

Now, I'm out front, pacing, pysching myself up. "Just do it," like the man on the commercial said.

I walk in. I felt like bozo the clown. Big square sunglasses. Baseball cap pulled down low. Humungous overcoat. Sawed-off shotgun. Brown wool gloves. Baggy pants. Satchel. Demand note. I was sweating. My heart was pounding. I approach the teller. She tells me, "Sir, I'm sorry, this window is closed. . ."

Now what? This wasn't in the plan! I felt like this was going to turn out like one of those Woody Allen movies!

Next window. The teller reads the note. Very explicit instructions. Short and to the point. "I want all the money, or else. . ." She studies me, after reading the note to ascertain if I am serious or not. I show her the shotgun. She knows I'm serious. (It was hanging over my shoulder by a camera strap. First and last time I ever took it into a bank.)

Then she starts stalling. I realize now that the alarms had already been tripped and she was stalling for time. At that time, I just thought she was scared and confused. She was a pro. I was the one scared and confused.

"Sir," she asks, "Where would you like the money from?"

"What kind of a question is that?" I asked myself. Now I'm really confused!

What does she mean. . ."Where do I want the money from???

She knew she had me. The switchboard at the police station was lit like a Christmas tree. Robbery in progress. . .

Meanwhile, back at the bank, I was being extremely patient. After all, Mom did teach us our manners. In another robbery the teller later commented on that in the police report. "He was very polite."

"Do you want the money from here?" (Pointing to the drawers beneath the counter in front of her) "Or, over there?" (Now pointing to the drive up window.)

This is where she gained control. I shrugged my shoulders. She went to the drive up window section, slowly and returned slowly with a pitiful stack of small bills. I was disappointed. This wasn't going according to plan. This isn't how it happens in the movies!

She placed the money on the counter. I stuffed it into my satchel.

Squad cars were rolling. En route. Code three.

It was a stand-off. She was testing me. "I said I want ALL the money." She opens a bottom drawer. My heart missed a beat. It was full, stuffed full of cash! The most money I've ever seen!

She removes one bundle. Locked the drawer, placed the bundle on the counter and steps back. Like, that's all you're getting, whether you like it or not.

I've been in the bank entirely too long as it is. The bundle felt a little peculiar when I picked it up and placed it in my satchel. In a few seconds I found out why.

It exploded when I walked out the door. At first I didn't know what it was. I thought they (the police) were shooting at me. It made a pretty good pop! (Like a gunshot)

Then I heard hissing. SSSSS. . . Like a flat tire. A pop, then hissing. Sounds like a blow-out to me. It was on a busy street.

Right when I thought I had figured it out, I was totally engulfed in red smoke! I started gagging too, because it was laced with tear gas.

I took off at a dead run towards my getaway vehicle. A bicycle. When I ran by the drive-up window there she was! The villain!

Now I was the victim trying to get away. I wish I had a video of it. "World's Funniest Video" would have paid some big bucks for this one!

I turned around and looked behind me to make sure nobody was following.

When we were kids some friends of ours had a pool. Their parents would put a chemical in the pool that would turn urine bright red. This way, at every party only one kid would pee in the pool. Suddenly, when said kid would be acting really calm and nonchalant, a red cloud would form around him. It was futile to swim away because the cloud would follow.

Well that's exactly what the red smoke did. Followed me right into the bushes!

I peeled the outer layer of clothes off and took off on my ten-speed. Font tire was slightly out of balance so I couldn't go too fast or I'd crash. I felt like a circus bear.

When I got home and looked in the mirror I was shocked! I had a slightly red tint to me. Whatever that stuff was, it wasn't coming off!

Next morning early, there was a loud persistent knock at the door. I peaked out. F.B.I.! I panicked. Grabbed my shotgun. I'm shootin' my way outta here!

My girlfriend says, "Wait a minute, wait just one minute. . .I'll handle this.! She comes back a couple minutes later with a "Watchtower" and an "Awake" pamphlet. I almost blasted two Jehovah's Witnesses!

Good Lord have mercy. I wasn't cut out for this line of work.

That cured me for a little while. But then I started have illusions of grandeur. I added a clause to my next note: "No exploding money, or else. . ."

* * * * * * *

Take care Dwight. I hope that all is well. If things get any better on this end I won't be able to stand it!

Respectfully
<u>Mike</u>

The Gang

*"I chastised myself for laughing so hard
at a potentially deadly crime."*

June 16, 1997

Dear Mike:

I just finished reading your last letter for about the fifth time. It was so intriguing to read your *Woody Allen* adventure. I enjoyed the story and description of events and then I chastised myself for laughing so hard at a potentially deadly crime you were involved in. But thank you for sharing it with me. Like you, I am grateful that neither you nor anyone else was ever seriously harmed. Is it unfair of me to ask for more? I would like to hear about the helicopter caper and perhaps several others that might be of particular intrigue or irony. Did you ever work with others? I can only imagine you have wonderful tales about interaction with others in such enterprises. You have described such wonderful characters including your buddies in the kitchen and the "man in the fan", that I relish getting to know some of the "gang". I don't want to push or offend so only give me what you are comfortable with. I am also anxious to hear more about Yak the seagull man (as you promised).

* * * * * * * *

Recently the TV has replayed the powerful movie *Shawshank Redemption*. It is a wonderful movie. I watched it twice. Obviously, it would remind me of you (not that you are digging an escape tunnel) and your relationships with fellow "cellies" and "mates". The most poignant parts were about inmates who had been in so long they were frightened to go back outside.

* * * * * * * *

They went in and drilled a hole through one of my vertebrae to make more room for a nerve that goes to my left leg. They also removed part of a disk to take pressure off the nerve. When I became conscious it was a great feeling to have the numbness and pain of the left leg gone. Probably part of the great feeling was also the residual effects of the drugs. Anyway, I have been convalescing at home and coming to work just part days while I recover. As I sat at home alone with nothing to do and feeling closed in I got another glimpse of what you deal with every day. It was maddening for me and I'm only talking about two or three days.

* * * * * * * *

Things are going extremely well in my life. My daughter, Juli, who was divorced last October found a wonderful young member of the church who was also divorced. I had the pleasure of performing their civil marriage on May 10th in Salt Lake City. It was fun. I knew as a bishop I would have an opportunity to perform marriages but I hadn't imagined my first one would be my own daughter. Our youngest son left on his mission to Baltimore as I mentioned and his older brother is still in Seattle so we are kept busy sending letters, money, and encouragement to both of them.

* * * * * * * *

Well my friend I will close. But I look forward to your next episode of Bank Robbery 101. Take care of yourself.

Dwight

Obnoxious Attorney: "So you say you never took his pulse?"

Coroner: "No."

Obnoxious Attorney: "Hopefully you weren't a total incompetent. Did you check his blood pressure?"

Coroner: "No."

Obnoxious Attorney: "Surely sir you must have checked other vital signs"

Coroner: "No."

Obnoxious Attorney: "Aha! So you can't even be sure that he is dead, can you?"

Coroner: "Well I have his brain in a jar but I suppose he could be out practicing law somewhere."

Get Well Card

"Vrooooooooooommmmmmmmmm."

June 29, 1997

Dear Dwight:

This is the closest I can come to a "get well" card. I wish a speedy recovery so you can get back on that bike.

Respectfully
Mike

Chop and Yak

"An escape is a cure. What would one not undergo to be cured?"

July 21, 1997

Dear Dwight:

How he acquired the nickname is unknown to me. Maybe because he chopped his eye out in an elaborate escape attempt that failed. His getaway driver didn't show up. Not to change the subject, but this is why I always worked alone. I could rely on myself. But more on this later.

Meanwhile, back to "Chop." He spent 23 years trying to get away from the 'belly of the beast." He even succeeded a few times, but never lasted long. Just added more time to his sentence.

His first attempt I know of (and he had some stories) is when he either slashed with a razorblade or gouged out his own eye with a pencil. I've heard both versions. The plan was to get to the outside hospital where his girlfriend was supposed to be waiting with guns and a getaway vehicle. She never showed. Can you imagine how "Chop" must've felt? Can you even imagine mutilating yourself in such a manner? Not I. It just goes to show how much this man wanted his freedom.

Years later he finds a way out through the sewer system via a storm drain. Only problem is, the storm drain is buried beneath a pile of coal that has been continuously piled high and shoveled for years. In fact, that was his job at the time. Shoveling coal. This is how he made the discovery.

The weight of the coal over the years made the ground level sink. The coal was right on top of the storm drain. So it never completely drained. It stayed full of water year round. I would draw a picture, but I don't want the oppressors' to get the wrong impression. So I'll just do my best with words.

They didn't know how far they had to go under water until they were free. In fact, they had no idea what was on the other end. So they filled some plastic five gallon milk bladders from the chow hall with air and went for it. They made their own crude scuba gear in other words. And it worked!

From the maintenance building they stole a hydraulic jack. In order to do this they had to make a replacement for it. All tools must be accounted for before any prisoner leaves his work area. They did so with cardboard, paint, convict ingenuity and patience. One thing we learn in prison is patience.

The jack was used to spread the bars at the other end of the storm drain. The exit. It worked. They got away.

But can you imagine what it would be like crawling through a storm drain totally submerged in total darkness with a limited air supply not knowing what was at the other end?

* * * * * * * *

The most important part of an escape is what are you going to do once you get away. Once again. As the years drag on people forget about us. That's the beauty of prison. See? I can <u>always</u> find a bright side. The beauty is, you find out who your friends are for real. You lose contacts. And the longer you are in prison, the more people fear us when we get out.

They didn't have much going and were apprehended shortly thereafter. Most likely involved in some petty crimes.

Now, they were returned to THE maximum security federal penitentiary at the time. Alcatraz had been shut down. So they were in Marion, Illinois.

They could make a movie out of this one: Tower #1, the main gun tower was having problems with the control panel. He is the one who lets visitors, employees, etc, into the prison by running them through a series of five gates. All electronically controlled by him, monitored with cameras.

The problem was minor. So they decided to fix it there at the prison's electric shop.

It was supposed to be a big secret. The convicts found out about it anyway and went to work.

They acquired all the necessary schematics and figured out exactly what they needed to by-pass the entire electrical system. And started smuggling in the parts. "Chop" said he was in the visiting room swallowing resistors, transmitters, etc. . .etc. . . Some of which didn't go down very easily.

"If they were hard to swallow, what about the other end Chop?" He just smiled. .

* * * * * * * *

Anyway, they now have everything they need. And they all five enroll in the "Writers Club." And patiently await the circuit board. This all took several months, but in "convict-time" is nothing.

The panel arrives. They know exactly what to do. Even under intense supervision the convicts were able to install all the necessary components in all the right places. The guard had no idea what they were doing, in other words. He was watching them, but he didn't know what he was watching for! What's the deputies name on Mayberry R.F.D.? Barney Fife? Well, the B.O.P is full of them! As you well know just from your brief encounter!

All the parts are in place and the panel is returned to tower #1. Where "Barney" turns a couple screws and all is well. So they think. . .

Until the "Writers' Club" had their annual meeting in the visiting room Wednesday night.

"Chop" and the boys were ready. The meeting was in progress. Everybodys' attention was focused on the "outside guests." The guard was apprehended, bound and gagged, and locked in a broom closet, unbeknownst to the guests!

The main cable was tapped into where the 9 volt "override" was installed. A remote control TV changer. When the appropriate switch (button) was activated, all five doors started opening simultaneously.

An alarm immediately alerted the man in the tower. Something's seriously wrong! He hit his override. Both overrides were straining against each other. It was a power struggle. The Writer's Club meeting continued completely unaware of what was happening. The guard in the tower couldn't reach the phone. "Chop" and the boys knew this. They knew it was just a matter of moments now.

When the guard let go of his emergency override to summon help, all five doors to freedom crashed open so hard, three of them jumped right off the track! Five desperate men ran right out the front gate, into the parking lot and commandeered a vehicle.

The chase was on. Three were captured almost immediately. Two ran into the woods. One of which was captured later.

"Chop" got away on top of a semi tractor-trailer rig all the way to Chicago, in the dead of winter. He said he never knew what wind chill factor was until that night.

Sometime in the wee hours of morning, he climbed down into the sleeper compartment and ate the driver's lunch and drank his coffee.

That's right about the time the driver decides he's hungry. Reaches back and feels "Chop" instead!

Now Chop is a big man. Over six feet, 240 <u>solid</u> pounds, shaved head, with a patch over one eye. Can you imagine having him crawl out of your sleeper compartment? Especially with that one evil eye locked in on you? He wore glasses too. Thick glasses. So it really intensified that one eye!

In fact, enclosed is a photo of "Chop." Once you get to know him, and he's hard to get next to; deep down inside, he's really a good person.

He made it to Canada. I forget how long he was out. Not long enough.

When he was apprehended he busted out again. Broke out of a Canadian jail and took off through the snow with plastic slippers on. No socks. They caught him. All they did was follow his footsteps. Pulled right up alongside him on a snow mobile. Asked'em, "What took you guys so long. . ? My feet were getting cold!"

He did 23 years total. When his day came, know what he told me?

"I don't want to go. All my friends are here."

* * * * * * * *

"Yak" was a nice guy. Somewhat docile and favorably inclined. Perhaps a tad bit "unbalanced" so-to-speak, but other than that, you couldn't say an unkind word about the guy.

He was like The Bird Man of J-unit.

The story goes something like this, and I regret that I wasn't there to see it with my own eyes because if you knew both parties involved, the story would have more, much much more impact.

Yak was kind of a loner. He was happiest when alone with his pet that he was convalescing and nurturing back to health. He'd develop quite a bond with the injured bird. He would sleep with them, eat with them, and shower with them. He'd carry on in-depth conversations with them. And you know what? The bird, would listen.

You know what they say about people that are a little "touched" in the head and their ability to, how do you say. . .communicate with animals? Well, it's true.

Yak was assigned to the "yard crew". This way he could take his bird to the yard with him every day, all day.

They would just walk around and mind their own business.

Well, there just so happened to be an overzealous "Hack" (slang for guard) that just couldn't stand to see a convict happy or minding his own business.

I know of this particular Hack too. This is what makes the story so beautiful. He had it coming!

There was Yak, happy and minding his own business. Sittin' on a bench rocking up soaking up the morning sunshine.

This guard kept provoking him. The guys on the crew kept telling the guard, "Hey. . .why don't you just leave the guy alone. . ." etc. . .etc. And so on.

The guard kept it up. And finally succeeded in ruffling Yak's feathers.

Yak come flying off that bench with some kind of war cry. He's part Indian, part crazy, part bird.

The guard is literally caught off guard. Doesn't know what to think as Yak is rushing him!

Pow!!! Straight right upper-cut to the jaw! The guard is air-born and lands on his butt. Stunned. This is when Yak starts working him! Left-hook, right-hook, left-hook, right-hook; the convicts were cheering! This is the part I would have loved to have seen! You know how some people just have it coming? Well, this guard had it coming. He loved making our lives miserable.

Somehow he hits "the device". His body alarm. Summoning help. Officer needs assistance! And boy do they come running! Thirty, Forty, Fifty deep!

They pull Yak up off the Hack and body slams him. Then pile on top of him about ten deep. Ever see a fumble on the one yard line in a play-off game? Well, that's what it looks like. We're the football.

Now there is some symbolism here that I'm not quite sure what it is yet.

In the lining of his jacket, Yak had a duck. The duck went down with Yak. When they body slammed Yak, they killed the duck. They said it was an ugly duck too. Wasn't quite right in the head. . .

* * * * * * * *

Should I behave for the remainder of my time, my release date is April 1st, 2001.

Should I get the halfway house, it will put me out right before Christmas 2000.

After ten, eleven, twelve years, six months either way doesn't make that much difference to me. However, the sooner I can get on with my life, the better. Even if it's one day!

Dwight, as always, it's nice to hear from you. I hope you get this letter. They may subject it to some <u>intense</u> scrutiny first.

* * * * * * *

Til then, take care. Let me know how your back is recovering. Also, it is always nice hearing good news! All is well here as can be. . .

Til the next time,
Your Friend
<u>Mike</u>

True Story?

"The clerk turned the robber down because he said he couldn't open the cash register without a food order. The man ordered onion rings."

August 12, 1997

Dear Mike:

I begin by telling you I now have two more heroes; Yak and Chop. I thought I was tough riding in ten below driving snow on a motorcycle in the top of the Rockies. But I was fully clothed and covered with boots, helmet, coats, extra socks etc. My hat is of to the champ, Chop! Imagine riding on the top of a rig with a 70 mile wind chill all the way to Chicago. Whew! Also his courage in the sewer line. I am so claustrophobic I get chills just thinking about it. As you said, "what would one not undergo to be cured?" Chop is a man's man. No one would question Chop's courage. . .his decision making?. . .maybe. . . but never his courage.

* * * * * * * *

I laughed at your description of Yak's catastrophe, then I chastised myself for laughing, and then I laughed again. I know it was serious for Yak. Losing one's duck is serious business, even if it is ugly.

* * * * * * * *

I trust Yak has recovered and found a suitable replacement bird.

* * * * * * * *

The Ann Arbor News crime column reported that a walked into a Burger King in Ypsilanti, Michigan at 7:50 am, flashed a gun and demanded cash. The clerk turned him down because he said he couldn't open the cash register without a food order. When the man ordered onion rings, the clerk said they weren't available for breakfast. The man, frustrated, walked away. Do you really think this is a true story or is it one you guys have heard a hundred times?

* * * * * * *

I took the motorcycle in to the shop the other day because the clutch has been slipping more and more. As you know it simply will not do to 'punch' the throttle and not have an appropriate response (interpreted to mean "a head-snapping acceleration that gets me around a truck in a nano-second). I mean, if one is riding for fun then it better darn well be fun. . .right?

Some people love ducks. I love motorcycles. What can I say?

* * * * * * *

I read the Book of Mormon every day for thirty minutes during my lunch period. It has a profound effect on me. As I serve as a bishop and deal with peoples lives I am sobered at the iniquity and problems people seem determined to bring into their lives. I deeply wish some of these kids would listen more attentively to counsel. Sometimes I wish I had you here to talk to some of them.

* * * * * * *

My back is improving steadily and I hope to be back on the basketball court in about two more months. In the meantime I have obtained a small overhang just above where I buckle my belt.

Dwight

Robbery Disguise

"I must've looked like a bucktooth beaver when I walked in."

September 17, 1997

Dear Dwight:

A brief update on "Yak" before I take you into my next bank.

They, "the bureau", sent Yak to Springfield, Missouri, (Springfield is the official Nuthouse for the Federal System) for psychiatric evaluations. Which was totally unnecessary because everybody already knows he is crazy.

He gets there, first night, he's tired. Finally gets a cell. Lies down. Something pokes him in the back. There's a "shank" poking through his mattress. He beats on the door with it, summons a guard, turns it in, falls back to sleep.

Several hours later, they rush him in his sleep. Find two more shanks (prison knives) in his mattress!

That's a serious offense. They charge him with it and send him back to U.S.P. Lompoc.

He's got seventeen years to go. I wonder if he's going to make it? So far he has three knives, one guard, and one dead duck on his hands!

* * * * * * * *

Bank Robbery 101: continued. Think I'll be punished in some way for glorifying these events?

* * * * * * * *

It was perfect. And it went something like this:

It was a Friday night, finally. I had been working hard all week. Ten, sometimes twelve hours a day, sunup to sundown. It was dark when I went to work, and dark when I got home.

I was stalking roofs in the middle of summer. Brutal, mindless and savage work. Up and down those rooftops all day long. 100+degrees. Moving tons of material. Tons and tons of material.

It didn't matter. I wanted to do the right thing. I was making an honest living.

All I wanted to do was get home, take my boots off, take a shower and relax.

I got home. I'm hungry. I'm thirsty. I'm tired. DAWG tired.

The stereo is blasting! The house, actually a very small studio apartment is packed full of degenerates. The party has been going on for hours. I'll spare you the details, but the place was in shambles.

The refrigerator had been raided. There was nothing left. I had not one nice thing to say to anyone. So I said nothing.

I went to take my shower. When I came out the place was empty except, of course, for all the empty beer bottles, etc. And my girlfriend who was standing there with her hands on her hips, tapping her foot.

"You're such an *@!*##", she said. "Why can't you be more sociable?"

That was it. The final straw. I snapped. I had been struggling to maintain my composure, but every man has his limit. I had just been pushed beyond mine.

I snatched her up by the throat and pinned her against the wall. I've never hit a woman in my life, so instead, I punch the wall.

CRACK!!! No. . .it was more like. . .SNAP!!! I hit a stud. The wall didn't budge. I broke my hand. Boxer's fracture is what they called it at the hospital. And of course, they wanted to know how I did it.

I lied. They knew it, but fixed it anyway.

I drove myself home, wondering, "Now what?"

My little $349.00 check didn't last very long with no more coming in.

I had to make a decision, and had to make it fast. It was the following Friday. It was now or never. Banks would be closed on the weekend.

I called the doctor and told him I need a new cast. Mine got wet.

"One minute please", said the secretary. I held my breath. "Mr. Taylor, will 3:30 be O.K.?" Whew. . . "Three-thirty will be perfect!"

Now I had to move fast. Got out the tin snips and removed the cast from my right hand and forearm. Then bound it up best I could with duct tape.

Put on a long sleeve shirt, some weight-lifting gloves. The kind with the fingers cut out so it wouldn't be real obvious. Wearing gloves into the bank in summer looks suspicious. Then painted my finger-tips with clear finger-nail polish. Several layers. Acts like an invisible glove so you don't leave any prints behind.

I put on a wig and a false mustache. A long haired wig. And a baseball cap. Some sunglasses. And false teeth. Which really distorted my facial structure. I even put some cotton in my cheeks.

I must've looked like a bucktooth beaver when I walked in.

I handed her the note: It said some really terrible things. Poor girl was scared. It was obvious, but they are trained not to resist. She asked me something. I forget what is was. It didn't matter. I couldn't answer anyway. The false teeth and cotton would have fallen out! So I just stared at her. I think this is what scared her most. The grunting noise, like a caveman. Poor thing. She got the message and started moving.

So did I. My getaway which once again was a bicycle. I distinctly remember how dry my mouth was. The cotton balls in my cheeks sucked all the moisture out! Plus, I couldn't close my mouth all the way because of the over bite. So the wind didn't help matters much.

The gloves I might add were to conceal the duct tape on my right hand.

Traffic was excruciatingly slow and snarled for some reason. I was weaving right through it with the greatest of ease. Long hair flying, buck teeth and chipmunk cheeks. The adrenaline was flowing. My legs were pumping!

* * * * * * * *

Now I'm thinking, "Wow! I just got away with it!"

I ran up the back stairs after ditching the getaway vehicle. You can stash a bicycle just about anywhere! (Even under the stairs!)

Hastily, I strip my disguise off. Who shows up? My girlfriend's sister! Bad timing! She keeps her pre-occupied while I clean up and get ready for the doctor.

Here they come. From every direction. I didn't know this town had so many police. It was a major event!

I drove calmly through the roadblock, right past the bank, ten minutes after they were robbed, on the way to the doctor's office.

Got my new cast put on and stopped at the grocery store on the way home.

The cashier was really excited. She told me all about THE BIG BANK ROBBERY that happened that day, in broad daylight! (She knew more about it than I did!)

* * * * * * *

Your Friend
<u>Mike</u>

Surprise Visit

"My wife and I paid a surprise visit to
Mike while we were in Phoenix"

October 16, 1997

Dear Mike:

Well we made it home. As we flew over Arizona and Utah it was inspiring to see. We crossed the Grand Canyon and the sky was clear so we could see from horizon to horizon. I could see Phoenix on the south and southern Utah on the north. What beautiful country.

* * * * * * * *

I don't have much to say because we caught up on all the news and answered your last letter during my visit.

* * * * * * * *

It is important to me you know how much I treasure being able to visit with you. This last visit was as exciting to me as the first. I didn't make any new friends with your guards but then I didn't have much time to chat with them. It was fun to surprise you. Keep me posted about transfers and anything else good that happens in your life.

Dwight

Transfer Approved

". . .one step closer to home."

November 17, 1997

Dear Dwight:

I'm excited! I may very well be there by time you get this letter. We're just waiting for the bus.

* * * * * * * *

Think about it. Free room and board. No responsibilities. Almost every decision is made for me. What to eat. What time to eat. The list goes on.

* * * * * * * *

I came to this conclusion today. The fences and gun towers are not to keep us in. They are there to keep people out! Just kidding of course. Don't tell "them" (the oppressors) I said that. They might let me go!

* * * * * * * *

Dwight, I feel as though I am cutting you short this time. I'll make it up to you. I promise. Stay tuned. There's more.

Mike

Christmas

*"May God's peace be with you in your solitude as you
look out through the bars this Christmas night."*

December 20, 1997

Dear Mike:

You made it to Tucson. Congratulations!

* * * * * * * *

I called the facility to make sure you were there. A women answered
and I asked her if I could send you a Christmas gift.

She said, "No gifts!"

I said, "How about some books?"

"No, only if they come direct from the publisher."

"How about some clothes?"

"No clothes!"

"How about some Christmas candy or food?"

"No food!"

"How about a computer?"

Pause, "loud laughter. . ."

"Isn't there anything I can send?"

"A letter."

"I mean for Christmas."

"Money."

"How?"

"A postal money order."

"Thank you very much, Merry Christmas."

"Yeh…..(click)"

* * * * * * * *

So here is a postal money order. I had two twenty dollar bills (you have
to pay cash for a postal money order) and there was an eighty-five cent charge.

Thus the money order in the strange amount of $39.15. Sorry it is so impersonal and cold. Anyway, it comes with love and the spirit of the season.

* * * * * * *

I laughed at your comments about oppressors letting you go if they knew how well off you are. There was an item on the e-mail that was almost word for word of your letter. Here it is.

In prison you spend the majority of your time in an 8x10 cell.

At work you spend most of your time in a 6x8 cubicle.

In prison you get three meals a day.

At work you get a break for one meal and you have to pay for it.

In prison you get time off for good behavior.

At work you get rewarded for good behavior with more work.

In prison you can watch TV and play games.

At work you get fired for watching TV and playing games.

In prison a guard locks and unlocks, opens and closes the doors for you.

At work you must carry a security card and open doors yourself.

In prison you have your own toilet.

At work you have to share.

In prison they allow you to visit your family and friends.

At work you can't even speak to family and friends.

In prison all expenses are paid by taxpayers, with no work required.

At work you get to pay all the expenses to go to work plus pay taxes.

In prison you spend most of your life looking through bars wanting to get out.

At work you spend your time wanting to go inside bars.

In prison you can join many programs which you can leave at any time.

At work there are some programs you can never get out of.

In prison there are wardens and guards.

At work we call them managers and supervisors.

* * * * * * *

A couple of months ago I hired a new computer person named Mary Dickson. She got married, had three children, and then her husband abused them and finally left. She had the courage to go back to school and to teach herself about computers. She basically lifted herself up by her own boots. An amazing woman with lots of courage. She loves working here and feels her life is improving each day. I took the liberty to let her read some of your letters (I hope that was ok) and she sent me the following e-mail.

Hi Dwight.

I just wanted to thank you again. The words you exchanged with Michael and his responses touched my soul. He's been through so much, seen so many horrors, and yet continues to try and improve, finds beauty in little things around him, and looks for opportunity where others give up. I found myself looking at my little ones differently this morning. . .I have them for such a short time, and their choices may take them down paths I shudder to think of, yet it is now that I have the chance to influence, to love, and to teach.

I'm afraid I've been caught up in the rush of earning the living, keeping the home, trying to figure out all the logistics of "making it". I've been neglecting their little personalities, their emotional needs. I will do better.

Thank you. Thank you. And thank Michael. For the perspective. For the lesson in gratitude. And for the message of hope.

Mary.

See, you continue to have positive influence over others. You life "inside" is not a waste but rather an inspiration to others because of your attitude and courage.

* * * * * * *

Yesterday I had a biopsy to determine if there is cancer in the prostate. I will get the answer next Monday (keep a good thought). My wife, Linda, was telling her boss about it and mistakenly said Dwight had just been to get an "autopsy". Whoa! Suddenly a biopsy doesn't seem so bad. They had a good laugh at her office. I know I'm boring but I wonder if that was some type of a Freudian slip (wishful thinking) on her part. Now that I think about it, she didn't seem too distressed with the autopsy announcement. Hmmmm. It's true that I have a good insurance package and. . . . . . . perish the thought.

* * * * * * *

On a brighter note, we retrieved our son from the mission in Seattle. It was a great trip and we enjoyed his companionship. He talked constantly, telling us of all his contacts and experiences. We met some of his Vietnamese converts and heard their miracle stories. As we drove west out of Seattle and reached the mountain pass we passed a sign that indicated the elevation. This is the boundary of his mission. He was chattering along and then suddenly said, "Hey, we just left my mission". Then he was quiet. We glanced over to see a tear. That was our confirmation he had been a faithful and dedicated missionary.

* * * * * * *

Well, I have to go get some decorations ready for the invasion of the grandkids. Eighteen kids (ages 3-9) will be to our home over the next few days. Afterward, Linda and I will smile at each other, thank Heavenly Father for all our blessings, and then start mucking out the place and trying to restore it to its warm and cozy form. Probably food in the carpet will be the hardest to clean. Linda and I keep reminding each other that kids are more important than carpet.

* * * * * * *

Dwight

Thank you Lord

And sort of a chill, more like a tingling sensa-
tion ran through my body. It was like a response of
some sort. (Has that ever happened to you?)

January 19, 1998

Dear Dwight:

I want to thank you very, very, much for the wonderful Christmas gift! That was totally unexpected and a very pleasant surprise.

* * * * * * *

I was running and feeling pretty good while absorbing the beauty that surrounded me. I said, "Thank you Lord for this previous moment. I never ask you for much, but this one time, please let Dwight be alright." And sort of a chill, more like a tingling sensation ran through my body. It was like a response of some sort. (Has that ever happened to you?)

* * * * * * *

They, the police force are a million strong. They work in shifts. They wear you down. Being an outlaw is probably the hardest thing I've ever done. It's a twenty-four hour a day job, seven days a week. It's relentless. Especially with today's technology. There's no where to hide. And once you're on the run, there's no turning back. Suddenly you are alone. You become the man from no where. No friends. No family. It's a tough way to make a living.

Sure. It's glamorous for a brief moment. But suddenly the shine wears off, and you want to go home. But you can't.

* * * * * * *

My "celly", "Bodies-by-Bear" gives me all the space I need. He's hardly ever here? He goes way out of his way to make sure I get all the study time I need.

His real name is Raymond Self. I've known him for years. But goes by "Bear". He tried to shake the "Bear" handle when we transferred here. But wherever you go in this system, there's always somebody who knows you.

So he tells me, "I'm introducing myself as Ray when we get there." First thing when we get on the bus leaving Phoenix a guy in the back shouts, "Hey Bear!"

"Bear" looks at me and says, "So much for that. . ."

I call him "Bodies-by-Bear" because he's constantly working out. That's how he does his time.

And he's done enough time, he knows how to act. A convict in other words. A dying breed no doubt. We just shake our heads in wonder as we watch this new generation coming in. The Pepsi generation. They're helpless! But I'm [sure] that's what they said about me twenty-four years ago when I started.

* * * * * * *

Stay tuned. Love. <u>Mike</u>

Master Chef/Waste Treatment Engineer

"Dealing with the situation at both ends."

February 25, 1998

Dear Mike:

Your last letter was fun for me to read again. It was also sobering. You caught me off guard. I was reading merrily along and when I got to the part where you told me you had said a prayer for the first time in a long time I really was thrilled. My brain was rushing ahead of my reading and I wanted to know what you had prayed about. I read your words about "please Heaven Father let". . .and then I saw my own name. I wasn't prepared for that. I was wondering what prayer you would be asking for yourself or if you were giving a prayer of thanks for how things were going for you, or some such thing. But to see that your first prayer in some time was for someone else, that someone else being me, I stopped reading. You talked about the feeling you had (tingling) and wondered if I had that feeling. The answer is yes. I have had that feeling many times and I had it again at that moment. My feet started to buzz and the feeling immediately rushed right up to my head and came out my eyes in the form of tears and I couldn't see to read any more.

* * * * * * * *

It sounds like you have a new celly that is compatible. Hello to "Bear".

* * * * * * * *

You're now back in the kitchen eh? I guess your chef reputation serves you well. It occurs to me that you could come out of that place with a very humorous and unique skill combination. I can see it on your resume now "**Master Chef/ Waste Treatment Engineer.**" That would keep them guessing wouldn't it?

* * * * * * * *

Dwight

Another Bank Robbery

"I did not anticipate a helicopter."

April 2, 1998

Dear Dwight:

Unfortunately "Bear" couldn't hang. He's requesting an immediate transfer back to Phoenix.

* * * * * * * *

There's a high concentration of people per square foot here. This is pre-trial detention center. That means there are prisoners running around that haven't even been sentenced yet! This is the only place in the country that does it. Mixes sentenced with unsentenced prisoners.

It's hard on those of us who have been around awhile. These guys don't even know how to behave. They haven't been schooled yet on the do's and don'ts of prison life. They haven't seen anybody stabbed repeatedly for cutting in the chow line. I've seen enough stabbing to last me a life time.

* * * * * * * *

I don't cut in front of anybody. Did I tell you about the time the helicopter followed me? I was carrying a transponder and didn't know it. That was close! They were hovering practically overhead while I was in the house counting the money.

I'll always remember that particular one because of the look the teller gave me. It was a <u>hard</u> look! And she didn't appreciate me robbing <u>her</u> bank.

She was a veteran. She had been around awhile. If you're going to rob a bank, try and get a young, inexperienced teller. One that doesn't know the tricks yet.

She slipped me a bundle of old tattered one dollar bills. The last ones you count. I heard the helicopter hovering overhead before I even got to them.

Sure enough. There it was! About the size of my watch crystal. And they were getting their coordinates, because I could "feel" them closing in.

So I gave the transponder to Sue (of course the names have been changed to protect the innocent) and told her, "Get rid of this!"

It worked. When she left, so did they. So they, the Federalies were very close that time.

It wasn't very well planned out either. It was more spontaneous then anything.

My getaway was a mountain bike. The bank was perched up on a hill, near a bicycle path, along a river with a foot-bridge spanning the river. I parked my pickup on the other side of the river. The getaway was all downhill. So nobody on foot had a chance. And a car could only follow me as far as the bridge.

That was my philosophy anyway. I did not anticipate a helicopter however. It's pretty hard to outrun a helicopter.

I learned about transponders that day.

* * * * * * * *

Then it was "on the road again" for me, going nowhere, fast.

* * * * * * * *

The story of my capture is still forthcoming. I haven't forgotten. I'll <u>never</u> forget that day. The dust. The heat. The shotgun butt to the base of the skull. "It's over Mike. . .don't make us kill you. . ." I'll never forget those words either.

* * * * * * * *

Your Friend, Mike

A Pretty Good Life

"Unfortunately, the free agency element of the plan of salvation means that all of us get rained on."

April 17, 1998

Dear Mike:

I was sorry to hear that "Bear" couldn't hang. But I understand. Sometimes mental work is the hardest work in the world.

* * * * * * *

I enjoyed visualizing the transponder story. You didn't say if your decoy, Sue, got away as well. I presume she did. Isn't technology wonderful?

* * * * * * *

In answer to your question about how I and your father carry such a heavy load, that is be involved in so many things, the answer is simple. We bag the social life. That is also how we pay tithing. No expensive nights on the town.

* * * * * * *

Living righteously doesn't guarantee a perfect life here – just hereafter. However, it also makes for a pretty good life here as well, even if we have problems and sickness. Thanks again for your concern. I am a happy man.

* * * * * * *

Most of my children are doing well. They claim they love me. I now have 25 grandchildren with one more on the way (that we know of). My work is satisfying and challenging. I have my health. I have faith. I have freedom. What more could a guy ask for? I even have sufficient income for my needs. I pray your life will also continue it's upward trend. We ought to start making some plans to spend a week doing something you would like to do after you get out.

* * * * * * *

Dwight

"Ouch!"

"He's not the sharpest knife in the drawer."

April 22, 1998

Dear Mike:

I know this letter is out of our usual sequence but I thought you might enjoy these items that came to me across the internet. Maybe they are old jokes to you – if so enjoy the reruns.

* * * * * * *

- ➢ "Someone broke in and stole my security system."
- ➢ "The take was so small that the burglar tied up the clerk and worked the counter for three more hours."
- ➢ When the detectives asked the men in the line-up to say, "Give me all your money or I'll shoot," one man shouted, "That's not what I said!"
- ➢ Panic makes us act in strange ways: "Doctor, my wife's contractions are only two minutes apart!" "Is this her first child" the doctor asked?" No, you idiot! This is her husband!"
- ➢ While robbing a bank in Modesto, California, the man simulated a gun in his pocket with his thumb and finger. He became flustered and failed to keep his hand in his pocket.

Dwight

Self Improvement

"I never had any idea how beautiful a scruffy old cactus can become. What was just a scraggly old barren stick in the ground a month or two ago has blossomed into an extravaganza of floral beauty. Reds, yellow, oranges, like I've never seen before."

May 21, 1998

Dear Dwight:

If you want to improve your circumstances, first you must improve yourself. There is no easy way. With forge, fire and flame, I do not intend to pause or rest or rust...just keep moving forward. You and my Father have really become an inspiration to me. It's truly amazing the amount of energy you two have:

"Do not follow where
The path may lead.
Go instead where there is
No path and leave a trail." - unknown

* * * * * * * *

Life is beautiful and I'm surrounded by it. Things are looking brighter every day. I'm just staying focused on my school. Next thing you know, I'll be outta here! As early as Christmas 2000 now.
April 1st, 2001 at the latest. That is if I can control myself.

* * * * * * * *

I'm seething from an earlier incident so I moved to another place to study. Along comes an orderly (a janitor) who decides he <u>must</u> clean right where I am sitting.
He starts tipping tables up. I'm already mad. It's the way he went about it that provoked me to say something I should not have said. Think

before you speak, right? Well. . .it was too late. What was said was said. Of course he took offense. And in turn, as I was walking away, he said something that offended me. When I spun around, he was shaking his fist at me. I went for him. A friend grabbed me. "C'mon Mike. . .he ain't worth it."

* * * * * * * *

Mike

P.S. You <u>are</u> cleared for visits: So if you're in the neighborhood: Here's the hours.
SAT. SUN. HOLIDAYS: 8:30 AM-3:30 PM
MON. TUES. 5:30 PM – 8:30 PM

Your Friend, Mike

"Anger"

"It is never satisfied nor is it satisfying."

June 16, 1998

Dear Mike:

I just finished re-reading your May letter. It made me extremely nervous for you. I'm so grateful you had the courage to walk away.

* * * * * * * *

Well we have had some excitement around here lately. Two separate instances of wild west shoot 'em up. A bank robber everyone in the west was looking for came into our little city of Provo and robbed a couple of banks. Our campus BYU policeman heard the call on the radio and suddenly found himself at the site of a robbery in progress. The gunmen saw him and turned and fired from ten feet away. The first bullet misfired apparently, (or missed). The officer dived into his car and the robber walked toward the police car and fired again. The bullet came through the windshield and hit the steering wheel and then ricocheted into the gut of the officer. It stung but didn't penetrate because the steering wheel had taken the major impact. He did get some cuts from the flying glass. The robber got away and was later put on the ten most wanted. He was captured in Las Vegas. The BYU officer survived with a great story to tell his grandchildren.

* * * * * * * *

The second event captured the nation's attention. Three fugitives shot and killed an officer and wounded two more in Cortez, Colorado. They then escaped into the wild country of the four corners (my home country). A friend of mine was taking his lunch break in a nearby small town and decided to drive out by the San Juan river to relax. He started to get out of his car when he saw a boot on a nearby horizon. He next saw a rifle barrel pointed at him. He slammed his foot to the accelerator and drove away as a bullet whizzed by. He informed the local sheriff's office. My cousin was the first officer on the scene. He looked around and then got out of his car. He also saw the boot (apparent place to draw attention and set up any curious person for target practice – pretty sick fugitives). He then saw the rifle barrel and turned to run back to his car. He was wearing a bullet proof vest, but the shooter was using armor piercing rounds and shot him in the back. He went down as the bullet pierced the vest and went through his shoulder. Then while he was lying on the ground the guy shot him again. It went through him just below his heart. When re-enforcement arrived they rescued my cousin and got him to the hospital where he survived. They went and found one of the three fugitives dead from either a self inflicted gunshot wound or from his buddies doing away with him. Neither of the other two were captured and seemed to have escaped. The whole thing was a fiasco. The Navajo Indian police were critical of how the search was handled. They think that they should have been more involved because they know the country extremely well. The Navajo people reported seeing a suspect but the local sheriff said it was probably just one of the investigative team and never followed up. There is a theory that while the one guy was shooting at people the other two got on a conveyance and simply floated down the San Juan River out of reach of the search perimeter. It is extremely wild country and it would be hard to root out someone who knew the country and was prepared. Apparently the suspects knew the country and had stowed caches of food. That is the same country Butch Cassidy and the Sundance Kid used to hide out in. It is just like the robbers roost area that is seventy-five miles north. A little irony to this story as well. While my cousin was in the hospital at Grand Junction, Colorado, his wife was in the hospital at Cortez, Colorado, delivering another baby. He had planned to take her to the hospital immediately after he investigated the sighting. Life has strange twists.

* * * * * * * *

When you come to visit I want to take a couple of days and show you around the San Juan country. That area is about as free and wild as it gets.

I wish you continued good luck with your studies. Like you, I am starting to get excited about April 1, 2001.

Dwight

[This document came as an insert to Mike's next letter]

The Final Days

*"Everything was in slow motion now. That's
what happens right before you die."*

I knew it was going to end soon. You can feel them closing in. It now
was just a matter of time. But never in my wildest dreams did I dream it
would end like this.

It was August 26, 1990. Almost eight years ago to the day. Even
though I was in a methamphetamine psychosis, I remember the entire
episode as though it happed just yesterday.

I was with a girlfriend. We had just run out of drugs. I needed more.
My connection, "Doogie", (Doug Francis) had been missing for about
three days. Nobody seemed to know where he was. I was getting upset
and desperate. Psychological addiction is the worst kind. The mind is
powerful. When it tells you that you need something, you believe it. Especially when you have been consuming massive amounts of a powerful
mind-altering drug. Nothing else matters.

For three days and nights I called "Doogie" to no avail. Finally, at
10:20 A.M. Aug 26th, (don't know what day it was, in that state of mind
everything becomes a blur) I had my girlfriend call. She asked for Doug.
He hated the name "Doogie." When it was a girl calling, he came to the
phone.

"Where've you been Doogie?" I asked. You see, I had been robbing
banks already. And a good portion of the money was going directly to
him. And I had already paid him in advance for a considerable amount of
"crank" (methamphetamine). He vanished shortly thereafter. I figured he
was trying to burn me. This is when all reasoning stopped and pride took
over. In my mind, I was invincible.

I told him, "I'll be there in 20 minutes". He almost panicked! "No!.
No!", he said. There was a long pause. Obviously he was stalling for
time.

"What's wrong?" I asked. "Nothing. . .Nothing!? He was stressed. I could detect it in his voice. Then he said, "Meet me at "The Little Green Store" at noon.

"The Little Green Store. . .? At noon. . .? What's he talkin' about. . .?" I was thinking as I hung up the phone. He's never had me meet him anywhere. That's the last thing a drug dealer wants to do. Leave his house.

Immediately I knew something was wrong. The girl asked if she could go. I told her, "No, sumpin's wrong." I could feel it. I told her I'll be back in about an hour. I knew I'd never see her again as I drove off.

I had a '69 Coup de Ville all terrain Cadillac. A sawed-off Mosburg pump shot-gun. A handgun. A black cowboy hat. Levis. Cowboy Boots. And the stereo blasting: "I Can Feel it in the Air". By Phil Collins. Over and over and over again, I played that song as I checked my weapons. Shotgun loaded. Check. Handgun loaded. Check. I had been drinking too. Heavily. And just to "take the edge off," I was eating 10 mg Valium like they were candy. I cannot even begin to imagine a more deadly combination than that. Methamphetamines, downers and alcohol. Loaded guns. And my integrity had been challenged. I knew what he was up to. He was going to rob me! Ha! Ha! I laughed! We'll see about this! Turned the stereo up. Took another swig. Washed a couple more Valiums down. Weapon check. "Check". "Check."

I took all back roads. I was meeting him on the outskirts of Southwest Santa Rosa. All flat land out there. The South side is not the side of town you want your kids to grow up on. It's a rough neighborhood.

The closer I got, the louder the voices became. "Don't go!" Ha! I wouldn't listen. My intuition was screaming at me. I overrode all reasoning and pulled slowly, ever so slowly into the parking lot one hour late and he, Doogie, was still there! That's when the voice screamed, "Go!"

I stopped. In my rearview mirror I noticed a Sheriff's car pull out of sight around the corner. I shunned the warning. All warnings. Sheriff cars in this neighborhood are not unusual.

I slid my automatic in my back pocket. Took another long draw from my pig. And told myself, "Self. . .looks like it's time for a shootout at the O.K. Corral."

In my mind he was there for one reason. To rob me. He had seen me with large sums of cash. I thought he was going to try and deprive me of that.

I walked up to his truck. Hand on the butt of my pistol. I was ready. I was ten feet tall and bullet proof.

He was nervous. He was sweating profusely. I know it's hot. But he had sweat streaming down his forehead. He's partially bald. His eyes were wild. His knuckles were pure white from clenching the steering wheel of his '64 Chevy stepside pickup truck. Primer grey.

That's what I noticed. How nervous he was. He was not in control. I was.

"Where've you been D-O-O-G-I-E-?" Heavy emphasis on "Doogie." He hated that name.

"Uh. . .Uh. . .", he was searching. His eyes were scared. Something told me, "Pull your gun out, put it to the side of his head, pull the trigger."

That's when I noticed a blue I-ROC, 2-28 pull out of a little gravel driveway about 100 yards away, between some bushes. Then back up again.

"Where have you been?" I asked again.

He told me his truck broke down. "What was wrong with it?," I asked.

"The rear-end went out", he told me. So what do I do? I crawl up under his pick-up on that hot pavement that hot August afternoon. It was at least 100 degrees. And I was becoming a little irritable now. Especially when I crawled from underneath that truck.

"D-O-O-G-I-E. . ."(like when your mother catches you telling a lie) "That rear-end hasn't been touched." The bolts were covered with a thousand miles of road grease.

The IROC makes another appearance. Then disappears.

"What's goin' on Doogie? Got my stuff?"

"Uh. . .Uh. . .", searching for another way out. "Did you rob that Wells Fargo Bank in Fort Bragg?," he asks me as he turns his chest towards me. And sticks it way out.

"What?" I'm thinking to myself now something is really wrong. And it was.

"Doogie, did you see that?" As I point to the IROC backing up into the bushes again. And another Sheriff car pulls slowly around the corner.

Now things started happening. A Honda Civic pulls alongside us in the parking lot. A woman is driving. The man in the passenger seat is wearing headgear. Big headphones with a cord going down to his lap. She gets out of the car. She's tall. Short brunette hair. Attractive. And walks into the little market.

I walk over to the car... Knock on the window. My lawyer told me later, that's when they almost took you out the first time. You were in the cross-hairs. There was a S.W.A.T. team on standby. Doogie had told them, "They would never clear leather." I had intentions of going out "the hard way."

I knocked on the window and the man looks up at me. He too is surprised. His eyes get real wide! In his lap was a big black box with an antenna on it. His attention is focused on a meter of some sort. He's turning a black knob, trying to dial something in.

It still hadn't dawned on me he was trying to dial in on our conversation and Doogie was wearing a wire! I asked him, "What is that?" He wouldn't answer. Pointing at the box, I asked again, "Hey, what is that?" as he shoved it on the floor and tried to cover it up.

"Doogie, something is going on here. And I don't like it."

He was really nervous now. So when I asked him for the last time, "you got my stuff Doogie?", he panicked! He must've seen the gun in my back pocket when I approached the Honda Civic.

He told me, "it's at home in my little brown purse."

"What?" He was speaking down to his chest.

He told me to meet him at the old cement factory. A perfect place for an ambush.

"At the old cement factory?" I'm trying to make sense of all this.

He must've seen something wasn't right by the look in my eyes now. And repeated, loud, "I'm going to go get my LITTLE BROWN PURSE!"

That was his cry for help. Nobody moved. He drove off. Left me standing there. I walked into the store. The woman was standing there. An F.B.I. agent. She was just standing there. We both stood there. Looking at each other. Neither one spoke. Neither one moved.

The light comes on. Ping! I've been lured into a trap! Now I'm thinking how can I get out of it.

I can't believe what I did next. It makes no sense. I bought a sandwich. A deli-sandwich. A quart of milk. My last meal perhaps? I cut the line too. Out in front of everybody. It's funny how certain things stick in your mind.

I'll never forget the way she was looking at me. We didn't take our eyes off each other.

I walked out to my '69 Coup de Ville. Had just bought it two days ago for this moment. A premonition perhaps. Like I said, you know when the party is over.

I sat there momentarily savoring that poor-boy deli sandwich. Then slowly drove towards the IROC. I made eye contact with the two occupants because I stopped right directly in front of them, eating my sandwich. We all just sat there, looking at each other.

I was eating my sandwich, thinking, "if I had an AK-47 you two would be dead." And I smiled. And kept eating my sandwich. It was like a moment frozen in time. Like something you would see on an F.B.I. training film. Or one of those "Silence of the Lambs" psycho movies.

I drove off. Really slow. Nonchalantly. The Cadillac dies! I cannot believe it. There I am. One hundred yards away in a stalled car. This is how it ends?

Not hardly. I look in my mirror. There's one of the occupants of the IROC standing in the road with a shotgun. He is arguing. He's looking at me. Then at the IROC. He's confused. Doesn't know what to do. Looks like he wants to come after me, but someone's calling him back.

Of course he has no way of knowing my car died. He probably thinks I'm just waiting to see what their next move is going to be. They were being cautious because of what Doogie had told them.

"C'mon Baby. . ." I'm rubbing the dashboard. "C'mon Baby. . ." That big ol' engine is turning over slowly as I pump the throttle.

The F.B.I. agent runs back into the bushes. "Damn". I throw what's left of my sandwich out the window. Approaching, on the horizon are two white vans. What caught my attention was how slowly they were approaching. With extreme caution. In my mind I thought, "And death rides a pale horse."

An IROC pulls out behind me. Keeping their distance as the vans approach. It's the S.W.A.T. team that was lying in wait for me at the deserted concrete factory. They were called in for the kill.

One last chance. I knew it too. If she didn't start this time, it was over.

"C'mon Baby. . .please. . ." I rubbed the dashboard. Turned the key. She fired up! It was on! The chase was on! I left 'em in a cloud of black smoke!

Made a left turn. Peddle to the metal, then a right. Went through some stop signs in excess of one hundred mph. The country roads were long and straight. Laid out in a checkerboard pattern. Not too many places to go. I looked behind me. The IROC was just a blue dot now. I was laughing. That is until I saw the two white vans! I was confused. Where did they come from? They were moving diagonally into my path.

Coming across a levee or something. They were coordinating on their radius, cutting me off at the pass.

I made a U-turn. Never took my foot off the gas. I knew those vans were big time trouble. Way out of my league.

Now, I heading down the wrong side of the road, one hundred plus miles per hour, back the direction I came from. Heading straight for the blue IROC.

They exited their vehicle and ran, like they thought I had intentions of ramming them. That's what the police report read.

I made a few more evasive maneuvers to no avail. This is when the Coup de Ville became an all-terrain-vehicle. I was watching my mirror trying to establish the whereabouts of that blue dot. When I looked up, it was too late. The road made a 90 degree turn. I went straight through an iron gate into a field. Never slowed down.

Now I remember running parallel to a fence through a pasture. I had to get on the other side. The grass is always greener, right? I went through the fence, the long way, puncturing my radiator with a fence post. Back onto a road with barbed wire wrapped around my left front tire. It was an awesome sight to behold. They said I did this seven times. I don't remember. All I remember is those two white vans.

Back into another field. This time with the IROC on my tail. I went over a knoll, became airborne. Came down hard. Lost control. Started spinning just in time to see the IROC come over the knoll. I found out later when they came down, they never got back up. Their car was completely totaled. They watched me 'traverse the rough terrain at a high speed." As I made my last attempt. I wrecked into a culvert. But I must admit, that ol' Caddy made a good run. I was surprised what it could go over with enough momentum.

Now on foot I was scrambling for cover. I came to a large flood control channel. The Laguna del Santa Rosa. It was partially full. Mostly overflow from the wastewater treatment plant (Ironic, isn't it? That's where it all ended. And 11 years later, that might be where I start again!)

I waded into the channel. It was chest deep. Murky brown. And the banks were overgrown with shrubbery.

I crossed the canal. Went up the other side. Ran fifty yards, took my shirt off, and threw it as far as I could, then ran back in the opposite direction, back towards the "lagoon." Right before entering the water, I snapped off some dried cattails [they become hollow reeds when they dry out]. Entered the channel. Went west as far as I could until I heard the helicopter approaching. South bank, where the foliage was thickest.

I squirmed up under some tree roots that held me pinned to the bottom: and I proceeded to breathe through my two makeshift straws. There I remained submerged for three hours.

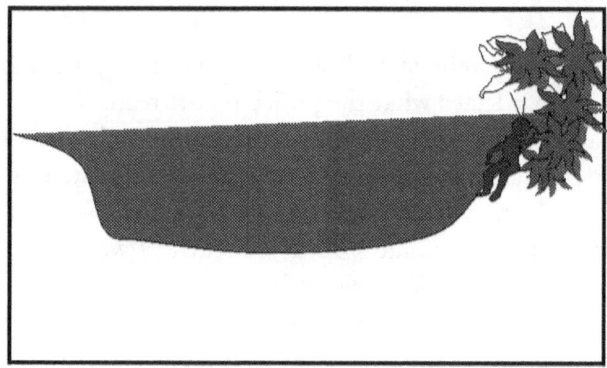

All I could hear was my heartbeat. And it was pounding in my chest after all the excitement.

R-e-l-a-x. . .R-e-l-a-x. . .I kept telling myself. The breathing was the hardest part. Inhale. . .r-e-l-a-x. . .exhale. . . Slowly I gained control.

I scooped muck from the bottom and smeared it on my face chest and arms, so I would blend in completely.

"Now, relax. You're going to be here awhile." I told myself. And this is when the first straw collapsed. It became soggy and failed! I inhaled some water! And came up choking! The branch/root that had me pinned to the bottom had a point on it that ripped the flesh on my upper chest as I scrambled for air.

They were everywhere! The helicopter was hovering dangerously low. I could hear men yelling to each other, beating the brush, looking for me.

My heart rate accelerated. With one straw now, I had to repeat the entire process.

Submerged once again, this is when I said that little prayer. "Lord, get me out of this one, and I'll go straight."

"When defenses against cold are not adequate, the result is hypothermia, a condition in which the core temperature falls below normal. The hypothalamus calls for an increase in skeletal muscle activity that leads to shivering. The word refers to rhythmic tremors in which the muscles contract about 10-20 times per second. Within a short time, heat production throughout the body increases several times over. Shivering comes at a high energy cost and is not affective for very long. . .In humans a droop of only a few degrees affects brain function and leads to confusion. . ."[1]

Needless to say, not only was I confused at this point, but almost totally incoherent. I crawled out of the water, up under the brush and like a cat curled up, I tried to get warm. It was futile.

It was 5:30 pm, at least that is what I think my watch read. All I could think about was getting warm. At the same time I was thinking, "just lie here until dark."

"The search had been called off. It appeared as though the suspect had got away!" That's what the police report read later.

Now the bushes all around me were shaking, I was shivering so hard. The accumulation of everything had taken its toll upon me. I was delirious [I had already started planning my next bank robbery. Told the Lord, "I tricked ya, didn't I?"].

I remembered seeing a barn. All I had to do was get to the barn. There would be a horse blanket there. I could curl up in the horse blanket and lie down in the straw until darkness set in.

Once again, I crossed the channel. I didn't remember it being this steep as I tried clambering up the embankment. I fell over backwards several times. I couldn't figure out what was wrong!

I crawled up the embankment on my hands and knees. Finally reached the top. Stood up, took three steps forward and slammed into the hard earth. I distinctly remember the dust.

Stood up. Fell. This time a little harder. Stayed down a little longer, trying to figure out why my legs were not working. My vision too was blurred. Everything seemed so bright, like an over exposed negative.

I rose to my hands and knees. My head was down. I was gasping for air, like a horse that had been run too hard. I looked at my chest. It was bleeding. But the dry dirt caked in the wound was helping.

---

1 Starr, Taggart: Biology, sixth edition 1992

I come up off the ground like a sprinter coming out of the starting blocks. This time the earth came up and slammed me in the face so hard I was rendered unconscious.

Don't know how long I was out but started dreaming. I heard my name being called way off in the distance somewhere.

"Mike. . .

. . .Mike. . ."

I didn't want to be disturbed.

"Mike. . .It's over. . .Don't make me kill you. . ."

"Don't make us kill you Mike!!!"

I opened my eyes. I was having trouble focusing.

Thirty feet in front of me there was a man, a sheriff down on one knee, with a 12 gauge shotgun pointed at me. It was an extremely intense moment. I was on my knees, trying to get up. The police report said I was told twenty to thirty times to lie down. The man's mouth was moving but I couldn't hear anything. The vein on his forehead was protruding. The veins in his neck were pulsating. The finger on the trigger was tightening. All was quiet now. "I need to get back to the swamp." That's what I was thinking.

To his right, about thirty feet was another sheriff. Same position. Down on one knee. He too was shouting something. Next to him, a K-9 unit. A dog, frothing at the mouth on a short leash. He was foaming at the mouth, in slow motion. Everything was in slow motion now. That's what happens right before you die. My vision was clear now. I looked at the man in the middle. He was tense. His trigger was pulled about half way back. He was leaning forward slightly anticipating the recoil. His mouth was no longer moving. I looked to my right. Thirty degrees. Another man down on one knee. He was shouting something. ". . .kill you. It's over Mike. . .don't. . .!!! silence.

I was trying to get up. Had I succeeded they would've shred me in the cross-fire. Mince meat hanging in the bushes. Had I gone for my gun, same scenario. It's a good thing I didn't go for it because I no longer had it!

To this day, and every day for the rest of my life, I'll never forget the look in that man's eyes, the one that was before me.

To the far right was another K-9 unit. They said there was three. I only remember two.

Our eyes locked again. The man before me and me. Then it happened. Some people laugh when I tell them this. So I'm careful who I tell it to. Some are fascinated. Others roll their eyes like, yeah. . .right.

I left my physical body. I was up above directly below the helicopter that was hovering silently and in slow motion. I remember the blades rotating right over head, counter clockwise, in slow motion. Everything was peaceful. Calm. Tranquil.

And I was watching what was going on down below. There I was on my knees, my Cadillac over there, in the ditch. The three sheriff's, down on one knee. They were close. There was more men running across the field, in suits, guns down. Those were F.B.I. agents. The two white vans, lurking on the perimeter.

What I didn't see was the blow to the base of the skull. The shotgun butt that rendered me unconscious. Once again, I was consumed by darkness.

When I woke up, it was from the pain. They lifted me by the hand-cuffs, and were stuffing me headfirst into the backseat of a patrol car. The sheriff that was in front of me, the intense one, leaned down real close and whispered in my ear, "I knew you were out there and I'm glad I got you."

I found out later he was a well decorated Vietnam vet, known for his bravery (or craziness) whatever you want to call it.

He waited for me. On his own time he came back and waited.

When I woke up again, I was face down, handcuffed on wet concrete. Completely naked.

It was over. That's what they were telling me. "It's over Mike. . .don't make us kill you. It's over. . ."

The Three Strike Law

"Jeopardized thousands of lives. If a man knows that he is going to prison for the rest of his life, he will go to extremes to get away."

July 17, 1998

Dear Dwight,

* * * * * * * *

I'm glad that your cousin is OK. My cousin was a sheriff up in Idaho. I'm not close to him. However, my aunt, (his mother, my dad's sister) and I are close. I can talk to her and she'll listen. I told her the general consensus (please excuse my spelling, somebody stole the dictionary from the library) of criminals, that is ex-cons being returned to society. Most are resuming a criminal career of some sort. Most are facing life without the possibility of parole if caught. Most say they're going to hold court right there. "Street-court." That is, shoot it out. And in order to do so, you must "get down first." This is what the three striker law has done.

* * * * * * * *

Please don't think I was glorifying my arrest. Eight years ago I was. My point of view has changed. There's absolutely nothing glamorous about the lifestyle. I know. I've been there.

* * * * * * * *

They gave me a second chance. It could have very easily gone either way.

Sometimes, let's see. . .how does that saying go? You don't even start to really appreciate life until you come face to face with death.

* * * * * * * *

With the most profound respect
Your Friend
Mike

"Tell Me About Yourself"

"I'm not so sure anyone has ever asked me to tell them about myself, so I don't know how."

August 29, 1998

Dear Mike:

Wow! What a story. I have re-read it a dozen times. Your "Final Days" capture story was exciting and scary.

* * * * * * *

I suppose when you tell the story you get different reactions. I'll share my reactions which may be a little different.

* * * * * * *

First of all I'm grateful you were not killed. An important chapter in my life would never have occurred if you weren't around.

* * * * * * *

Secondly, I definitely believe the hand of the Lord was in it. I take <u>very</u> seriously your near death experience (seeing the events from above), and I think that part of your experience deserves your serious contemplation. I wouldn't share it with anyone other than your parents and a few trusted friends. That is sacred and it will only be made fun of by others. In the scriptures the Lord talks about casting your pearls before swine, meaning don't give precious things to those who do not count them as precious. A swine would simply trample a pearl into the mire with no appreciation for its value. If I had such an experience I would treasure it and constantly pray about it and try to understand its meaning.

* * * * * * *

Third, I find it interesting that at the moment of your most desperate circumstance you turned to the Lord (I think that is embedded in every human that is ever born) and then abandon Him just as quickly when you thought you were going to get away. Fortunately for you He didn't abandon you. He allowed you to be captured alive and then has watched over you ever since. He did answer your first prayer, although not in the way you were anticipating.

* * * * * * * *

Fourth, I was shocked at what the drugs allowed you to do and how they affected your thinking. I've read all about drugs but somehow your story made me realize just how pernicious and evil that stuff is. It literally ruins lives. Most people ultimately die, don't they? You were indeed a lucky one.

* * * * * * * *

Finally, I was so pleased at your current attitude about the whole situation. When I read "Please don't think I was glorifying my arrest" and your other comments, I knew that you were seeing it CLEARLY now. I'm so pleased you have learned to enjoy much of your life, even though you are still confined behind fences. Fortunately, you have already escaped the real prison, the prison of a mind that wants to do evil. You have also escaped from the clutches of drugs. You are amazing.

* * * * * * * *

In closing I want to share a small experience with you, involving another prisoner (in for life). He had written a long letter asking that we change our records to show his middle name as the name of preference. So we did. I thought why is he making such a big deal out of this. Normally, I don't repond to letters from any of our 40,000 students [up to now you have been the single exception]. Our responses are generic and either handled by my staff or the computer. Anyway, I decided to drop a two sentence comment in a letter that was going back to him. I only wrote these words, "We have changed the records to show your middle name as the name for correspondence. By the way I would like to know a little about you if you would be willing (I also go by my middle name "Dwight"). That was all I said and I immediately forgot about it. A week later I received a personal letter which read, "First of all, thank you very much for not only taking care of the addition of my middle name, but especially handling it so promptly. Thank you Dwight! Next, I can't begin to tell you how your note, as short as it was, touched me. Just your interest or concern, <u>truly</u> touched me and I can't thank you enough for that! Your note was very encouraging, and that I am grateful for as well. You know <u>I'm not so sure</u>

anyone has ever asked me to tell them about myself [I added underline]. Because I don't believe I've been asked that before, it would be a little difficult to respond to".

He was unable to tell anything about himself. I was stunned by those words. Imagine that a fellow human being would live a lifetime without anyone every asking them about themselves. I keep thinking about that and feel so grateful that I am surrounded by those who care about me, come to visit me, ask about my welfare, and love me. Michael, I suspect that you are probably able to comprehend such a situation because you have seen so much of it. I can't! And it's been sobering for me to contemplate and ponder about. What a tragedy to live a life and no one even cares.

* * * * * * * *

I really want most of my letters to be a little more upbeat and cheerful. Please be patient with me when I get up on my soap box sometimes.

Dwight

The Light at the End of the Tunnel

"Dwight, I am getting excited. It's getting brighter."

September 21, 1998

Dear Dwight,

* * * * * * * *

This might sound a little strange, but I find a little ant hill fascinating now. I like to feed the birds and was looking at a cactus flower one day, up close. I've never seen one. They're beautiful. So I was looking at it. A guy walks by, observes me, and makes a snide remark to his friend: "Been down long?" and they both sniggered. Of course it was directed at me. He almost got slapped.

Then I had to remind myself why I am here. School. Stay focused. Little did he know I have watched guys get stabbed repeatedly with a sharp piece of steel for less.

* * * * * * * *

I'm glad you were able to appreciate my N.D.E. (Near Death Experience). I almost left that part out, fearing ridicule. (Not that you would ever ridicule me.)

* * * * * * * *

There's another time also. A time I actually went to "the white light," and came back. They were there. People I knew, with outstretched arms, clad in white robes, waiting to embrace me. I just had a chill run down my spine thinking about it. Perhaps I will tell you about it sometime if you are interested.

* * * * * * * *

In conclusion I would like to comment briefly on that other prisoners' response. You are right. Many are forgotten. This is their life. If you let

them out, they would either perish out of loneliness or commit another crime so they can come right back. I've seen it numerous times.
Your Friend
Mike

"I Am Ready"

"I Think."

October 16, 1998

Dear Mike:

* * * * * * * *

When you are comfortable I would appreciate the "white light" experience. We don't understand these things but I think it is small minded to ignore them or pretend something doesn't happen.

I was thinking about your experience last week. I was sitting in one of the many committee meetings I have to attend and started to feel faint. In a period of about five minutes I felt like I was going to lose it so I excused myself and called Linda. She came and rushed me to the hospital. They hooked my up to the EKG (heart monitoring equipment) and I could hear my heart beat. Three or four quick beats, then nothing for five seconds, then normal, and then rapid beating again. Doctors and nurses appeared from everywhere and were rushing around. They stuck a needle of something in my I.V. tube and suddenly the heart stabilized. I was laying there thinking, "I wonder if I'll have an experience like Mike had? I wonder if this is it. Not bad actually. I'm ready – I think. So this is how it is when you go." I was surprised at my own calmness and lack of fear that I might actually be checking out.

* * * * * * * *

Now for a report on our trip to Alaska. It was the best cruise I've been on. It was cold but thrilling. One of the many highlights was the helicopter Linda and I took to visit some glaciers.

* * * * * * * *

We would see chunks of ice the size of our ship fall into the ocean to become icebergs. It was truly awesome.

* * * * * * * *

I don't know what you are planning when you get out but I certainly plan to spend some time with you (after you have been with family of course). I don't know what freedom you will have but I would love to take you on a four-wheeling trip into the Canyonlands.

Dwight

Monster Test

"The instructor waited until a certain group turned in their tests. Then he left the room! I could not believe it.

November 23, 1998

Dear Dwight,

* * * * * * *

Due to the federal budget not passing on time, they shut us down temporarily. Unfortunately, right in the middle of some classes! So it took a minute to get the momentum going again.

First day back, we had a final exam. Then shortly thereafter, a mid-term presentation in "Humanities and the Environment". Followed by yet another final exam in "Intro to Haz Material." Which was an extremely boring topic. Nevertheless, it is required. So we must take the good with the bad.

The bad part was, the test was cumulative. One text.. No midterm. One shot at the grade.

The instructor let the class vote on it. "You guys want one test, or two?"

Of course they voted on one without thinking. Those are the guys that sit in the back and disrupt the rest of the class. They are the ones who don't care if they get a "C". (or D) Unfortunately, they far outnumber the ones who strive for that 4.0 G.P.A.

Needless to say, the exam was a monster as anticipated. The instructor waited until a certain group turned in their tests. Then he left the room! I could not believe it. Of course the ones who were allowed to cheat are the ones who voted for one test! At first it upset me tremendously. Then I cam to the conclusion, "Why?" After all, they are only cheating themselves.

* * * * * * *

One guy who just recently graduated from the program and is successfully completing (complying with) his parole, has just bought himself a new home, and a car. And has been out only six months! I love a success story. The guys that come right back crying about how hard it is out there didn't really want to make it to begin with. His base pay is $36K a year. Plus all the overtime he wants pushed him into the $51K bracket. That's not bad for a single guy coming right out of prison. And that's in Phoenix where the competition is fierce in this field.

* * * * * * *

My guard is up. I will not let anyone deprive me of what I have worked so hard to acquire.

You take care. I am looking forward to that four-wheeling trip into the Canyonlands. (Did they ever catch those two outlaws?)

Your Friend
Mike

"Christmas"

"Again. Still behind bars…"

December 12, 1998

Dear Mike:

* * * * * * * *

I just finished re-reading your last letter. It was full of enthusiasm for your schooling and anticipated future work. It's really exciting, isn't it, when we have something to look forward to and strive for. I think that is basically what life is all about.

* * * * * * * *

Two weeks ago I went to San Francisco to attend a conference.

* * * * * * * *

I got out the map and noticed we weren't too far south of Santa Rosa. Is that the place of your infamous run from the law? Anyway, I thought about you while we were there. One day soon you will be riding around that area yourself and having flashbacks as you visit the turf of your former life. Not too much longer aye?

* * * * * * * *

Those two fugitives were never found. Either they committed suicide, or died in the desert, or got away clean. No further trace of them. My cousin's boy has fully recovered from the gunshot wounds. He was lucky indeed. Did you happen to follow the story of the guy who escaped from Prison in Texas? He was the first to escape in over sixty years or something like that. Anyway his companions were quickly recaptured but they couldn't find him. Later he was found drowned in a nearby lake. The cardboard he had wrapped around himself so he could roll over the barbed wire around the compound, had soaked up the water when he jumped in to escape detection, and pulled him under.

* * * * * * *

I pray for you and I'm starting to feel the excitement you probably live with every day, of your anticipated release. In the meantime, buy yourself a Christmas present with this money order. God bless and Merry Christmas.

Dwight

Running Shoes

*"I will be running with two, possibly three of
the fastest young blacks in the prison."*
December 28, 1998

Dear Dwight,

* * * * * * * *

Thanks you very much Dwight. The money will be applied towards a
new pair of running shoes.

* * * * * * * *

They have what is called the Winter Sports Festival here. They approached me last night and asked me to run in the one mile relay. I will be
running with two, possibly three of the fastest young blacks in the prison.
It inflated my pride (and ego) a little to even be considered.

* * * * * * * *

I'll let you know how it goes.

Your Friend
Mike

Surprise Shakedown

"We're not supposed to know about it, but we do have a surprise shake-down coming this afternoon. It's kind of comical in a way."

January 20, 1999

Dear Dwight,

* * * * * * * *

Contraband in the penitentiary was "shanks", pieces of pipe, and other weapons of death and destruction. They didn't sweat the small things.

Here, on the other hand; heaven forbid if you have an extra pillow!

* * * * * * * *

Charlie just spent a week in the hole for having an extra pillow. Of course, it's not the pillow that placed him in the hole. It's what he said to the lady when she took it!

* * * * * * * *

San Francisco, huh? I have quite a few good memories associated with that city. Fisherman's Wharf, the Golden Gate, Haight Ashbury, Market Street. . .the list goes on.

Last time I was there was right after the Loma Prietta earthquake rocked the Bay Area.

I was up on the San Bruno Mountain watching the Goodyear Blimp leave the World Series. That's when I knew something was wrong. Harlen (my co-worker) and I had just come off of tower #3, done for the day. We were in the truck when the earthquake hit, so we didn't feel it.

We watched the blimp leave the World Series (Giants vs. Oakland A's) at Candlestick Park and fly to the Marina District, which was on fire.

Then we started picking up bits and pieces of the disaster on the radio. Then our boss called on the company radio and filled us in.

Only emergency vehicles were allowed in the area. It just so happened our truck said: "Tenco Towers, Communication Installation & Maintenance".

I asked the fireman at the barricade if his radio was working. He checked it. It was. I said, "Good, We have to go further into the city and set up communication relay."

He looked at the truck, (not knowing we were just some old tower hands) and lifted the barricade!

That was one of the strangest feelings I've ever had. Driving through San Francisco when it was blacked out and deserted. (Except for police, fire and National Guard.)

When we arrived at the Marina District there was a crowd of people who refused to leave. They had children trapped in a collapsed building.

Harlen and I looked like rescue workers in our hardhats and coveralls, equipped with flashlights and truck with radio.

There was a hysterical woman outside. You could hear her kids crying inside. I kicked the door. (We had the truck spotlight on it. One we used for climbing towers at night so it was pretty powerful). It barely budged but I got a murmur from the crowd as some rubble fell down around my shoulders.

I kicked the door again, harder this time. The building kind of settled on the doorjambs. It moved considerably this time. The crowd applauded. Now I was really pumped!

Third time was a success! I could now squeeze through the opening and emerged with two scared kids in my arms and the crowd went crazy!

"What a professional," I heard one of them say! The kids were crying and Mommy was crying and the crowd was cheering and everybody was happy. It's a moment I'll never forget.

In the wee hours of the morning, we rendezvoused with the boss at the epicenter. Santa Cruz mountains. (Loma Prietta.) We were trying to put KNTV, Channel 11, San Jose back on the air. Two hundred and forty-seven feet off the ground, at 3:00 A.M., the first aftershock hits: 5. (something). It was a ride I'll never forget!

Dwight, do you think we share some sort of personality disorder? I mean. . .we crave excitement, right?

I like the motorcycle. I showed it to "OKLAHOMA" (A.K.A. "Porky"). He really got a kick out of it! He thought it was real! Of course. . .what can you expect! After all, he is from OKLAHOMA! We tease him constantly. But then again. . . maybe the joke is on me! Maybe it is real!

* * * * * * * *

I have rambled on long enough. It's time for me to get ready for the surprise shakedown.

Hero at the San Francisco Earthquake

". . .and you never mentioned it!"

February 18, 1999

Dear Mike:

You always have these little surprises. Who would have known you were a hero at the San Francisco earthquake. We've visited face to face twice and you never mentioned it. You know I am afraid of heights and so your one sentence about riding the tower (several hundred feet in the air) while the earth was shaking really made my hair stand up. Just thinking about being that high on a tower would be more than I could stand. But to have it moving. . . . . . . .whew!!

* * * * * * * *

Remember my cousin who's son was a policeman in San Juan County and was shot twice by the fugitives? I believe I told you he recovered. His mother really had a tough time with that because she had another son at the same time who was struggling with depression and some business failures. Anyway, the other son disappeared a couple of months ago. His brother, the recovered police officer, found his pickup about a week ago in a secluded canyon and upon investigating found his brother's rotting body in a sleeping bag where he had crawled in and then put a gun to his head. I talked to the mother a few days ago and she is really having a tough time. The story is not complete yet because a third son was arrested and is now serving time for child abuse. Through all of the year while these three events were occurring she was in bed trying to recover from serious hip replacement surgery. Boy some people really get a load of trouble sometimes. The Navajo police recently started searching again for those fugitives after some reported sightings of footprints in some hidden canyons. I think those guy are long gone. Either that or they are professional survivalists. That is really rough country.

* * * * * * * *

I recently found out I am a final candidate for position of Dean of Continuing Education at Utah State University (USU) located in Logan Utah about two and a half hours north of Provo.

* * * * * * * *

In one of my more mischievous moments I thought I would use you as a reference. It probably would unsettle the search committee to see the following references.

Joe Osmeyer, Professor, BYU Instructional Science, Provo UT
Mentor

Terry Smithson, Businessman, Memory Publishing, SLC UT
Business partner

Michael Taylor, Inmate # 85227-011, Bureau of Prisons, Tucson AZ
Personal friend and associate.

* * * * * * * *

I am now two months away from my release as Bishop. I tell you Michael it has been the most glorious experience of my life. At the same time I am exhausted. It amazes me the decisions people will make and then walk in and expect the Bishop to solve all of their problems. We try of course, but the reality is we must all live with our own actions (as you well know). In fact we are all better off when we do own up to our actions and pay the consequences. *If we avoid the consequences we become scavengers. If we accept the consequences we become men.* I have some wonderful young men and women in the ward. I love them dearly and know the future of the church and the country is in good hands.

* * * * * * * *

Well, I've rambled more than usual. I think of you often. I'm extremely proud of your determination and focus to achieve. I hope you knock down the test and I look forward to your report. Tell Charlie whenever he gets out he can send me an I.O.U. and I will personally ship him a pillow.

Dwight

That Little Group was Waiting for Me

". . .they became highly upset. And turned it into a racial thing. Said, "We all bee in dis togetha Mike 'til you showed up."
March 17, 1999

Dear Dwight,

Have you ever had one of those days where everything went right?

Well. . .yesterday was one of those days! The results from our state exam came back. In fact, the licenses did too. And I am now the proud owner of a Water Treatment Grade III, Wastewater Treatment Grade III, and a Collections Grade II. All that work and stress for that little bitty license that must be "framed and displayed in a conspicuous place."

I don't know why I was stressing. Like you said, it's not the most important event in my life.

There was a certain group of individuals who refused to study. (Blacks primarily.) Who felt as though it was my obligation and duty to furnish them with the answers. When I told them "No", they became highly upset. And turned it into a racial thing. Said, "We all bee in dis togetha Mike 'til you showed up. . .etc." Bottom line is this. They were always able to pressure someone out of the answers through intimidation until I showed up.

I went to work that evening after the exam. Needless to say after five hours of intense testing (I was looking at it as my future at stake) I was exhausted.

Well, that little group was waiting for me because I said something to the effect of, "We'll deal with it after the exams." Sure enough, there they were. Seven, eight....maybe nine of 'em. And little ol' me.

I let 'em say what they had to say. Mostly hot air. If they wanted to jump, they had their golden opportunity, but I was not initialing a physical confrontation. After all, I am most like the one who would've been shipped straight back to Phoenix or worse yet, the penitentiary.

I came here for <u>me</u>. Not them! What part of this do they not understand? I came to class on time. I sit front and center. I do my homework. I study. My GPA is 4.0 and I'm proud of it. I refuse to look at someone elses paper during an exam. If I can't do it on my own, then what's the point? Is this selfish?

I guess I was just raised different. "That which is easily gained has little value." Like bank money. That which is obtained illegally that is, has very little value. It goes though your fingers like water. Mom always said I learn the hard way!

* * * * * * * *

The surprise shakedown went very well for me. Of course I don't have any major contraband. Just a few minor pleasures like a cushion for my chair, some extra underwear, that sort of thing. It's fun to hide it from them though. It gives me something to do.

Mike   *Your personal friend and associate, *I like that!

Wonderful Visit

"First and foremost: thank you very much for the wonderful visit!
I had to check with records to make sure I wasn't dreaming."

March 31, 1999

Dear Dwight,

Dwight, I'm on my way to class now. Take care. And once again,
thank you for the wonderful visit, and the moral support. It makes a big
difference when you know somebody out there cares.
Mike

Get In Line

". . .another corny joke.!"

April 19, 1999

Dear Mike:

First a report on our trip. We went from your place down to Tomb-stone and southern Arizona. We walked through the Boot Hill cemetery. Enjoyed it very much. Bisbee is really a neat town tucked away near the Mexico border. Then we went through Douglas, Arizona and over into a small insignificant town in New Mexico called Hachita. A few homes, some abandoned adobe homes, one public telephone, etc. No one would be interested in visiting there, except me. My grandfather's journals tell of how Pancho Villa raided, burned, and forced the Mexico Mormon settlers to leave Mexico and come back into the states for refuse. My ancestors spend a few weeks of wet muddy existence in a leaking tent in Hachita waiting for the opportunity, which never came, to return to their homes in Mexico. This was in 1912. Anyway it was fun to see the place which had a small part in my ancestral history.

* * * * * * * *

We drove to San Antonio the next day and spent the evening on the famous River Walk. It is a great cozy shopping and restaurant area located on the San Antonio River where it flows through and under downtown San Antonio. It is just a short walk from the Alamo.

The next day we made our way over to Houston where we spent the night. The following morning we picked up our missionary son, DuVall, and spent the day visiting with his converts and friends in the area. That evening we drove to Dallas. In Dallas we spent the morning visiting the site of the Kennedy shooting. It was sobering and fascinating. At noon we went to the Dallas temple and my son and his companion sat in as witnesses as a couple who had converted were sealed in the temple. They also had two daughters sealed to them. After the ceremony they hugged my son and thanked him with tears in their eyes for bringing them the gospel. It was a wonderful moment for me, the parent, to see what my son had done.

* * * * * * * *

I reread your account of the blacks who were angry because you wouldn't help them cheat. I'm glad you chose not to have a confrontation and that they didn't force one. Your dog-on-a-leash analogy was excellent. You asked what someone who has always been on a leash, like yourself, does when they are set free in the front yard. The answer is obvious. What you need to do is draw your own boundaries that you will not cross. Tough to do but imperative. Dr. Karl G. Maeser, one of the early founders and president of Brigham Young University said,

I have been asked what I mean by *word of honor.* I will tell you. Place me behind prison walls---walls of stone ever so high, ever so thick, reaching ever so far into the ground---there is a possibility that in some way or another I may escape; but stand me on the floor and draw *a chalk line* around me and have me give my *word of honor* never to cross it. Can I get out of the circle? No. Never! **I'd die first!**

* * * * * * * *

Let me conclude with a really corny joke. Hope you haven't heard it before. Tom was on the side of the road and noticed an unusual funeral procession approaching the cemetery. A long, black hearse was followed by another long black hearse about fifty feet back. Behind the second hearse was a solitary man walking a pit bull on a leash. Behind the pit bull were two hundred men walking single file. Tom respectfully approached the man walking the dog and said, "Sir, I know now is a bad time to disturb you, but I've never seen a funeral like this. Whose funeral is it?" The man replied, "Well, that first hearse is for my wife." "What happened to her?" "My dog bit her, and she died." Tom inquired further, "Well, who is in the second hearse?" The man answered, "My mother-in-law. She was trying to help my wife when the dog turned and bit her, and she died." A poignant and thoughtful moment of silence passed between the two men. Tom asked, "Sir, could I borrow that dog?" He replied, "Get in line."

* * * * * * * *

I am pleased at your enthusiasm for getting out. I suppose if I make one more visit next year, then the following year would be to pick you up rather than leave you there.

Dwight

Who Got the Money?

"During one of my robberies somebody (an employee most likely) pocketed $1,742.00. They too had a nice weekend at my expense."

May 16, 1999

Dear Dwight,

* * * * * * *

I really like the excerpt you sent me (included in your letter that is) about "Word of Honor". I'm going to record it in my chrestomathy and use it from time to time if you don't mind.

You are absolutely right Dwight. I am going to have to draw some boundaries I will not cross. And give my Word of Honor to myself that I will not cross them. Thank you for the positive feedback.

* * * * * * *

My parents were in Tombstone exactly one week after you! My father was describing the tombstones to me, but I really didn't grasp the total concept until you sent me the photos:

"Here Lies Lester Moore, Four slugs from a 44, No Less, No More." [he drew a picture of a light bulb] Ping! The lights come on! No less ... No more! Les is with us no more! Hey. . .now I know why my parents call me "SON" . . cuz I'm sooo bright!

* * * * * * *

And leave you with a joke: The LAPD (Los Angeles Police Dept.), the FBI and the CIA are all trying to prove they are the best at apprehending criminals. The president decides to give them a test. He releases a rabbit into a forest and has each of them try to catch it.

The CIA goes in. They place animal informants throughout the forest. They question all plant and mineral witnesses. After three months of extensive investigation they conclude rabbits do not exist.

The FBI goes in. After two weeks with no leads they burn the forest, killing everything in it, including the rabbit, and they make no apologies. The rabbit had it coming.

Then the LAPD goes in. They come out two hours later with a badly beaten raccoon. The raccoon is yelling: "Okay! Okay! I'm a rabbit! I'm a rabbit!"

OK ... OK ... enough already! I'm enjoying this correspondence as you can see.

* * * * * * *

Mike

Doc, What Do I Do If I Get That Feeling Again?

"Nothing. You're dead..!"

June 16, 1999

Dear Mike:

I'm glad to be here . . . in fact I'm glad to be alive. Last Wednesday I went in for an electrophysiology (EP). They send five tubes into your heart, two through the left groin, two through the right groin, and one through the neck. They map out the firing of the sinods to determine why the heart is having a tachychardia (irregular heartbeat or arrythmia). I was having problems with that several times during the past few months. On one occasion they had me in the critical care unit because it wouldn't slow down. They finally shot a needle into me that stopped the heart. Wow! The most incredible, depressing, terrifying, feeling of doom that one could imagine. It only lasted for about 5 seconds but it did the trick and my heart returned to a normal heartbeat. I asked the doctor what action I should take if I ever had that feeling again. He said, no need to do anything, you're dead!

* * * * * * * *

After reading your letter again, I got a chuckled about the bank employee who used your heist as a perfect excuse to pocket some take-home money, and a good size chunk at that. That's what you get for leaving some behind. I thought a pro like you would have cleaned the place out.

* * * * * * * *

Your CIA/FBI/LAPD rabbit joke is really funny, probably because there is some truth buried in there somewhere. That's what makes most humor work, it's uncomfortableness. I'll close with a few. . .hope I haven't already sent them.

How to write a carefully worded recommendation for a fired employee: Think about them.

The chronically absent:
> A man like him is hard to find.
> It seemed her career was just taking off.

The office drunk:
> I feel his real talent is wasted here.
> We generally found him loaded with work.
> Every hour with him was a happy hour.

The lazy worker:
> He could not care less about the number of hours he had to put in.
> You would indeed be fortunate to get this person to work for you.

For the unproductive whose job is better left unfilled:
> I can assure you that no person would be better for the job.

For the employee who you really shouldn't hire:
> I would urge you to waste no time in making this candidate an offer.

When you get out and go for your first job interview for water treatment make sure that any reference letters you have don't have these type of double meaning comments.

* * * * * * *

Dwight

Spirits Are Up

"I always feel better after writing."

July 30, 1999

Dear Dwight,

* * * * * * * *

That heart stuff (I can't even pronounce those words) sounds pretty scary! I'm truly amazed at modern technology.

* * * * * * * *

My spirits are up! I think I might even take your advice on some kids. Settle down some. Enjoy life. My parents are telling me the same thing. Had I only listened 25 years ago! Story of my life! If we only knew then, what we know now   ...

Thanx for listening Dwight. I'm very fortunate to have a friend and a confident such as you.

Mike

My Life Has Unraveled a Bit

"The tumor is cancerous."

August 16, 1999

Dear Mike:

I told you all about the heart thing and my plans to go to Seattle for a conference, and then a motorcycle trip with my daughter to see my other daughter in Minot. Anyway while in Seattle standing in front of the group giving my presentation, my left arm went numb and fell to my side. I completed my presentation and then found an immediate flight to Provo. The doctors were looking for a reason and concluded it wasn't heart related, but found a lump in my throat.

I had surgery and the tumor was cancerous.

* * * * * * * *

Anyway, the motorcycle trip was cancelled and I have been in and out of doctors' offices and hospitals for the past two months. Today I am at work for a few hours. Part of my planning (which is still very tentative – and dependent upon my recover) is to visit some high schools in New Mexico and Tucson around the first of November. If that works I might have a chance to come and see you again.

* * * * * * * *

Dwight

Phi Theta Kappa

" I'm being inducted! Is it a scam?"

September 20, 1999

Dear Dwight,

Hope you're feeling better. You must have a lot on your mind right about now.

Things are pretty quiet on this end. I'm just cruising right along ducking and weaving any potential problem I may see looming on the horizon. An old convict taught me that trick: "Anticipate a problem and avoid it. " I've lived by those words for nine years and it has worked.

For example, if you know somebody is getting their throat cut in the movie theater tonight, well then, it's a good night to stay home. Our theater was notorious for that back at the USFI (United States Penitentiary).

* * * * * * * *

I am being inducted into "Phi Theta Kappa", the international honor society for two year college students. What do you think Dwight? Have you ever heard of them? Is it a scam? Or do you think it would look good in a resume? I earned it. I'm proud of it. Why not? I figure every little bit will help. And I'm going to need all the help I can get!

My parents will be here next week. Sunday the 26th to be exact. As always I look forward to that. I told them this will be my last Christmas, my last Super bowl, and quite possibly my last Thanksgiving here. FOREVER! Enough is enough already!

* * * * * * * *

Please keep me posted on your progress. It must be a real scary time for you. Be strong. You're in my prayers. Please take care of yourself and I will do the same. Until the next time, with love and respect.

<u>Mike</u>

A New Discipline

"It's all right to allow others to earn a few credits to serve you."

October 2, 1999

This letter came as a surprise from Mike's parents.

Dear Dwight:

* * * * * * * *

Cynthia and I are greatly indebted to you for the special interest you have shown and the council you have given to Michael. With your crowded schedule I can't begin to imagine how you managed letters and visits. If there is any good come from Mike's experience, it will come from your genuine concern, encouragement and expectations. In his own way he is triumphing over adversity. I have faith Michael will succeed after his release, in a large part as a result of your expectations.

* * * * * * * *

Cynthia and I will remember you in our prayers. When the opportunity presents itself we hope to meet you and thank you in person.

Best Regards

Gerald Taylor

Radioactive

"Hey, Dad. Can you change the street light by blinking at it? Hee Hee."

October 22, 1999

Dear Cynthia, Gerald, and Mike:

Perhaps you are all mildly surprised with that salutation. I received a wonderful letter from California shortly after hearing from Mike and decided, in this one instance, I could write you all together.

* * * * * * * *

The counsel in your letter, Gerald, was absolutely on target. Thank you for the wisdom and understanding. You're right about me. I don't like depending on anything or anyone. It is a character flaw. I'm slowly learning the hard way. Of course I have depended on the Savior my entire lifetime and I depend on him now (Oh how I depend on him). With my track record I am totally at his mercy and grace. Thank you again. I'm so pleased you would take time to write to me. The timing was perfect. The day I read it I was in terrible distress with this cancer thing. They had put me in what is called "hypothyroid". In lay terms, and based on my own experience, it means they try to kill you before the cancer does.

* * * * * * * *

Here is the theory. Certain areas of the body demands iodine the thyroid produces. They took out my cancerous thyroid, then took away my thyroid pills. The thyroid areas (i.e. the areas where the cancer was) starts screaming for thyroid-iodine. At the point where you start to loose your hair, memory, muscle control and eyesight, and your face becomes puffy and pale the doctors have you drink iodine. It's like saying to the cancerous areas, "Here is some iodine. Help yourself." The catch is this, the iodine is radioactive. Whoooeee! The cancer areas, and *only* those areas, gobble up all the iodine and the radioactive stuff kills the cancer. Slick huh?

As soon as I was hypothyroid (see explanation above) they put me in an isolated room in the hospital. They hang a radioactive sign on your door and prohibit any visitors. Then they walk in pushing what looks like a overhead projector table, only it is made of ½ inch plate steel. It had a round receptacle in the middle about the size that would hold a thermos bottle. In it is a steel bottle with a rounded top (R2D2?) Then they back out of the room and call out instructions to you. "Turn the top off the rounded container. See the small bottle inside? Use the plastic device laying on the table to remove the lid from the little bottle. Good. Now carefully pick up the little bottle and drink the radioactive-iodized content."

Right!!!!!

I felt like I was participating in an execution.......my own.

* * * * * * * *

After my radioactivity went through several half-lives they came in with a device and measured me. The level was sufficient low to let me go home. I was in isolation at home for another three days. I endured the sick humor of my family during that time. Such comments as, "Hey, dad could you turn on the TV in your room by just blinking at it?" "Did you light up your room all night?" "Could you warm your food with your eyes?" "Could you see through the wall?" When I would touch them they would make a screwy ZZZZZiiiiiiip sound and act like they had been shocked. Anyway, they all handled it with typical family sympathy, sensitivity, and tenderness.

I got in a few shots myself. I handed my one son a few burnt peanuts (its a peanut that has a hard, bright red, lumpy bumpy candy shell, and is one of my favorites). After he had taken them I said, "Those were Boston Baked Beans before I touched them." He yelped!

* * * * * * * *

The middle of November I might just visit New Mexico high schools and sneak over to Tucson one day. We shall see. Maybe I'll still have enough radioactivity in my system to set off all the alarms at your place Mike. Wouldn't that be fun?

* * * * * * * *

Thanks to you all for the good wishes, prayers, and thoughtful correspondence.

Dwight

Y2K

*"What if it wipes out all records and I have
to start over! (Not funny Mike!)"*

November 21, 1999

Dear Dwight,

How nice it is to hear from you. I'm glad the operation and treatment went well.

That is some pretty scary stuff. The "C" word is always frightening. I attribute your speedy recovery to good living, good family support, and of course, prayer too.

* * * * * * *

I want to get out of here. I want to get to know my son. I want to meet my daughter whom I've never met. I want to be there for my parents, who have always stood by me no matter what. And I want to live a good life. The best revenge is living a good life.

* * * * * * *

Sometime in December when I attend my six month review ("Team") I should have a better idea of the exact date of release. Within thirty days (plus or minus). I anticipate it will be early November 2000. Six months in a half way house maximum will set me almost totally free by April 2001.

* * * * * * *

Mike

P.S. My parents were ecstatic to hear from you. They always ask about you. Take care

Dwight!

Guess What?

"they all know the answer. "You love me."

December 15, 1999

Dear Mike:

I knew I would be a little late getting you this letter. I suspect it will arrive *after* Christmas. Sorry. But let me be the first to wish you a Happy New Year. I teach the Gospel Doctrine Adult Class in church and have spent considerable time on the past couple of lessons focused on the mission and gift of the Savior. He died that we will all be resurrected. He also died that we can have hope and constantly seeks, and receive, forgiveness.

* * * * * * *

As I prepared the lessons I thought of you on several occasions. You are incarcerated and unable to enjoy the freedoms the rest of us have. My heart aches for you. I'll also think of you on Christmas Eve when I am surrounded by my mob of kids and grandkids. We expect about 35 to come. We have a tradition that each family has a talent number they share and then we exchange and open name gifts. It is a lot of fun and you can imagine how I feel as the patriarch of such a clan. I usual sit in a chair where I can grab the kids as they come by and give them hugs. I whisper in their ear while I'm hugging them, "Guess what?" I've done it for so long that they all know the answer. "You love me." I respond with, "That's right!"

* * * * * * *

I should tell you I also have times of extreme joy and happiness when I am alone. When I am riding my motorcycle, or walking across campus, or strolling through the park, or on my knees in formal prayer, I have such experiences. It seems to me that, even in prison, you could have such moments. Communion with God is personal, private, and beyond the bounds men may set. Everyone is free to do that. I trust, and hope you have found that to be true. God bless you.

* * * * * * *

Dwight

End of the World

"Now he and his family have to eat all that army surplus macaroni and cheese. 800 lbs' of it!"

January 19, 2000

Dear Dwight,

Here we are. . . the nineteenth day of the two thousandth year. . .and all is well. The world didn't end after all.

One of the oppressors here was so sure it was going to be the end, he took his entire family up into the hills in a secret bunker with thousands upon thousands of rounds of ammunition, tons of food, water, medication, a hand-crank radio, etc. . .and so on.

The other "oppressors" clowned him to no end. And to tell you the truth, I think he was a little upset when nothing happened. Or, he's just depressed because now he and his family have to eat all that army surplus macaroni and cheese.

* * * * * * * *

I'm about halfway through your manuscript also. What a great idea – a journal of your life. I happened to turn to the last page today inadvertently. There was a picture of the motorcycle! I cracked up!

I forgot all about that, I'm going to show it to some of the bikers here and tell 'em it's yours for real. You used to be a pilot, etc. And are still somewhat of a daredevil. And you are now getting ready to test drive it even as we speak. Hey. . .gotta have some fun right?

* * * * * * *

You mentioned as you prepared your lessons you thought of me on several occasions. "You are incarcerated and unable to enjoy the freedom the rest of us have. My heart aches for you."

That very touching excerpt brought to mind an excerpt I saved from one of my homework assignments from your literature course: "The pattern is that of the caged bird who, though captive, continues to sing. Despite his lack of "satisfaction", presumably of desire for flight and freedom, he knows joy." --Thomas Wolfe: "The Lost Boy."

* * * * * * *

Thanx to people like you, well not people like you, because there are not many people like you Dwight, because of you, (and my wonderful family) I know joy. You have become quite a positive inspiration to me.

Mike

My Temporary Hell

"When I am inside the top of the tube is about four inches from my nose. My arms are pressed tightly against my side and the tips of my shoes touch the tube lining."

February 15, 2000

Dear Mike:

My doctor told me, during my last visit, that I needed to go have another MRI.

* * * * * * * *

I have had several MRIs. They do this before performing back surgery, neck surgery, and cancer surgery.

* * * * * * * *

There is a problem, however, for anyone like me who is claustrophobic. The MRI is a circular tube that they stuff you in. I use the word *stuff* because it reminds me of being put into a sausage machine. When I am inside the top of the tube is about four inches from my nose. My arms are pressed tightly against my side and the tips of my shoes touch the tube lining if I let them relax and fall to the side. IT IS MADDENING! I usually takes about forty-five minutes. I come out sweating and only moments from loosing my mind. I simply cannot stand it.

* * * * * * * *

I think of you sitting in a small, confining, space from which you cannot escape and I wonder, "How can you do it?"

* * * * * * * *

I'm still chuckling about your *oppressor* that went out to wait for the end of the world. Give him a couple of tips from me. First, the end of the world is going to happen on Sunday. God is coming to see who is in church {just a joke}. Second, when the world ends everyone is going to be burned up, except the righteous {no joke}. So here is my advice for the oppressor. Spend more time and effort in turning yourself into a good person, and less time stockpiling.

* * * * * * *

I'm getting excited about a trip into the Canyonlands with you next year.

* * * * * * *

Dwight

Starter Kit

"A roll of duct-tape and a ski mask."

March 16,, 2000

Dear Dwight,

* * * * * * *

I was joking with my Mom about it (getting released to go home). She wanted to know who pays for my plane ticket. I told her, "They do, plus they give me $50.00 cash."

She said, "What can you do with $50.00?"

I said, "Buy a basic starter kit."

She said, "What's a starter kit?"

"A roll of duct-tape and a ski mask," I replied.

She started cracking up! And said, "Michael, I see you have not lost your sense of humor."

* * * * * * *

Well Dwight, that's about all for now.

Mike

Reality

*"I predict that the time will come when you dream of
the good old carefree days in the prison yards."*

April 13, 2000

Dear Mike:

* * * * * * * *

I've used your joke about the basic starter kit with all my family and
friends. They love it. One said, "He's kidding for sure, right?" I said, "Of
course. Mike's a professional. He would want the deluxe complete kit if
he went back into the business. A starter kit just wouldn't do." They all
laughed.

* * * * * * * *

Mike I am particular concerned for you. I have no doubt about your
desire to do things right when you get out, but things have changed. More
change in the world in the past ten years than in the preceding 4,000 years.
It's incredible. You are going to come out with high expectations and run
smack into the hum drum of everyday life. I hope you have the courage
to ride out the routine, unexciting, rudeness, and apathy that you will run
into in so many places. Life is tough, in or out of prison. The few nuggets
that we find along the way are a result of searching, persistence, patience,
obedience, and forgiveness. Most of the people out in the world are just
as unhappy as many incarcerated individuals. True, they are free, but they
don't know how to appreciate it or take advantage of it. They think they
have to be rich to be happy. They walk around in self made prisons.

Please come out prepared to be patience, forgiving, disappointed, but
determined to mine the nuggets.

* * * * * * * *

I predict the time will come, within the first year or so, you will have
times when you dream of the good old carefree days in the prison yards.
It will probably happen when you are sitting at the table trying to decide

which bill to pay and a baby is screaming in your ear while the wife is burning the casserole.

* * * * * * *

Dwight

Decisions

*"...the biggest decisions we have to make in pris-
on is what kind of ice cream to buy on commis-
sary night. All other decisions are made for us."*

May 17, 2000

Dear Dwight:

* * * * * * *

I was reading some more of your autobiography and that story about the time you and your friend were riding and you turned down that road to find that lake. . .and you knew something was wrong. . .just weren't sure what. . .that is scary! [My friend and I (Dwight) turned off a highway in remote northern Canada and road about a mile before we both got spooked. We got out of there fast] I've been there. In a similar situation that is. And it's scary. Especially when you're with somebody who picks up on the same "vibes." Makes you kinda wonder, doesn't it? Who's looking out for me?.

* * * * * * *

On Mother's Day we had our first annual 5K run, fast walk, walk. It was fun. I placed second in the 5K run. I came in fourteen seconds behind "RIP."

"RIP" is the fastest runner in the joint. I told you about him before. He must be part Kenyan! That guy can run!

He beat me by a full minute in a one mile race we had awhile back. So I was pretty proud to finish right on his heals in the 5K.

Next month I'm pushing for a 10K run. I think I can take him in a 10K. He's ten years younger than me too! People kept referring to me as, "you older guys. . ." (Don't you hate that?) I'll show 'em what "an older guy" can do next month! Ha!

* * * * * * *

Mike

Antsy

"The time gets closer."

June 20, 2000

Dear Mike:

I took a moment to reread your last letter. I must say I enjoy them over and over. I probably have reread your capture letter a dozen times. It still takes my breath away.

* * * * * * * *

I wish I could have watched you run the 5K. If you get to run the 10K I hope you can rip "Rip", you know, one for the old guys. Anyway it was fun to read your account of the race.

* * * * * * * *

Hey man, if you have finally figured out how to decide what type of ice cream would you mind sharing it with me. Just the other day Linda and I stood in front of the ice cream freezer at the grocery store and spent an agonizing several minutes trying to decided. We finally settled on Maple Nut because that is my favorite kind. We bought a half gallon but I didn't get to eat much of it. Next time I'll just buy her favorite flavor—if she can decide what it is. You could help me write a best seller. "How to Decide What Flavor of Ice Cream to Buy." Every man, woman, and child in the country could benefit from such a book.

* * * * * * * *

I have been hesitant to ask but if you are willing I would really like to hear one or two more of your bank robbery stories. If you would rather not, that is okay. Perhaps I'm starting to get too nosey but I would also like to know what you did with the money—in a general sense. Did you wait until you were broke to do it again or was it just the rush that motivated you? Were you a loner or did you always have some help? Are you at risk when you get released? Are some guys waiting for you to do you harm?

[He never answered this question but time would prove it relevant] Now you are getting close to being release I would be interested in your general state of mind. You said you have some objectives. Does that include looking up old buddies? Do you have any old scores to settle? Are you going to be okay?

* * * * * * *

—if you're willing to talk about it (your call).

* * * * * * *

Dwight

October 4th, 2000, San Francisco

"I could not help I ... had to just blurt it out!"

July 22, 2000

Dear Dwight:

* * * * * * * *

That's my release date from here: Destination, somewhere on Taylor Street. No kidding! Could this be a good omen? It's right smack in the middle of the tenderloin district i.e. the "RED-LIGHT" district. Know what I mean? Prostitution, drug addicts; etc., another Sodom and Gomorrah. Don't you just love it?

* * * * * * * *

I know ... my Dad is scratching his head too! [Michael was turned down on his request to be released to Sacramento where his family could be a support. Instead they sent him to the "tenderloin district."]

* * * * * * * *

So in 72 days (can you believe it?) the easy part is over: Prison. And then the true test will begin. Not only will I be subjected to some very intense scrutiny (supervision that closely resembles harassment), but I will also be exposed to everything that led to my demise. They have it all backwards. What I need more than anything else is to go to the mountains for a month. Somewhere quiet. Somewhere peaceful. Somewhere I can get back in touch with myself. With nature. With God.

* * * * * * * *

Maple Nut huh? I had forgotten about that one! That's my Mom's fav-o-rite one also! If I walk into, (No! when I walk into) a Baskin Robbins 31 Flavors ice cream parlor I might "short-out"! Information overload! I didn't even know where I'm going to start ... Pizza? Steak? Ice Cream? One thing's for sure: San Francisco sourdough. There' nothing like it!

* * * * * * * *

Let's see ... one or two more bank robbery stories...

* * * * * * * *

Here's one that sticks in my memory. The robbery itself was uneventful so-to- speak. Other than the fact the teller was intentionally slow-playing me. Stalling that is, and it was obvious. It was so close that while still in the bank I could hear sirens approaching from all directions.

The bank itself was near a shopping mall, but away from it. Kind of sitting there all by itself way out in a parking lot without much cover. I had a long way to go to get to my truck and I was on foot. When they (the police) asked the teller if she recognized any unusual characteristics about the suspect, she said, "yes, he took very long strides."

Well, of course I did! The PO-LEACE were coming! But I did not want to run either. That's a dead give away. Remember, "stay cool like the fish in the pool. . ."

There were some dumpsters about halfway between my truck and the bank. This is where I changed my clothes. Well, actually shucked a layer. I always wore two layers of clothing. This particular time I was wearing grey khaki-like pants over cut-offs. It was summer, so it was not unusual. I had on a white long sleeve shirt, a nice one, with a tie. That's the funny part. I sent the photo to my Mom later and she said, "That's not Mike. He never wears a tie." (Did I tell you this one already?) I had on a blond wig also, that I tucked up under a baseball cap with some long strands hanging out. I did this intentionally. I wanted it to appear that I was trying to conceal my long blond hair, but at the same time, I wanted them to see it. I had on a false mustache. Blond also. Very bushy. Again, I wanted it to stand out. I had on very lightly tinted sunglasses. Walking into a bank with sunglasses on is very obvious. The idea was not be extremely obvious, but try to distort your (my) eye color. That's one thing they always look at. Your eyes. One, to see if you are serious. Two, to determine the color. I know as a retired bank robber who used to insert colored contact lenses to throw them off. And third, when looking into someone's eyes, it establishes a height. Did you look up? Down? Or straight across? So the tinted shades were to distort the color of my eyes.

The sirens are loud now. My heart's pounding! I duck behind the dumpsters which are surrounded by wooden fences. I pull off the outer layer: Wig, mustache (that hurts!) glasses, shirt, tie and pants. Within seconds I'm completely transformed into somebody else, like Superman ducking into a phone booth. That's how I felt sometimes emerging.

Before entering the bank there were two vehicles parked near my truck. My truck was way out back behind the shopping mall. Again, isolated. No cover whatsoever. Not good positioning I learned later. You want to blend in. Not stand out. This is the reason. The two vehicles nearby were obviously involved in some sort of illicit activity. I suspect a drug transaction going down of some sort. So they were a little suspicious of me when I pulled up, maybe thirty yards away. They were checking me out needless to say.

I leave as a nicely dressed long-hair, and return as a poorly dressed short-hair. I noticed they were checking me out once again as I returned moments later. I tried my best to just ignore them and act nonchalant like, "Nuttin' happenin' here guys." Knowing that within minutes the place will be swarming with cops. City cops, county sheriffs, highway patrol, FBI., and they always bring out the helicopter! So who knows? I may have got these suspicious lookin' scoundrels busted! Ha! Ha! I didn't even think of that until just now! Because if I was a cop, I would have checked them out anyway just for general principle, bank robbery or no bank robbery!

Now it gets good: And to answer your next question, what I did with the money. I would go straight to the connection. My drug connection, and buy massive amounts of drugs. Methaphetomines. I had it bad. While at the connections' house, I run into Bonnie. A girlfriend of an old girlfriend. She tells me her aunt is out of town, why don't I come over for awhile?

Sure ... why not. We go to her aunt's house. We're there maybe an hour at the most. The phone rings.   She answers it. She's doing more listening than talking. Just keeps saying "mmm ... ah ... huh...ah ... huh..." Like, "O.K.. . .1 understand."

Then she says, "Why don't you come over. There's somebody here I want you to meet." And hangs up.

About thirty minutes later, who walks in the door? The two tellers from the bank I had just robbed hours ago!

They both get a really good look at me in the bank too, because the one teller I handed the note to, handed it over to the other teller who in turn was looking me over trying to remember every detail.

I recognized them immediately. Is this a small town coincidence or a set up? I remained calm ... didn't even flinch, as Bonnie made the appropriate introductions.

The one I robbed, couldn't take her eyes off me all night. She was studying me very intently Dwight. And even made a startling comment during some casual conversation as the evening progressed.

I was doing something and she said, "I work at City Bank (Citibank)." I didn't react or respond in anyway. In fact, I acted like I didn't hear her and continued what I was doing.

Again, this time even louder, and more clear she repeated, "I work at Citibank." She was looking for a reaction. I know it. This time I looked up, directly into their eyes, and smiled, and said, "Oh ... that's nice." Never once did either one mention the robbery.

Later, when they finally left, Bonnie and I went for a walk. It was 3:00 am and I asked her about her two friends. She said one really liked me, but the other one said there's something about him ... I can't quite figure it out ... but there's something about him... it's like she knew me from somewhere. just couldn't quite put her finger on it. ... but she was close!

* * * * * * * *

Am I at any risk when I am released? No. Only we can diminish ourselves. But to answer your question, there's nobody waiting to do me harm. All I ever did was take the banks' money, federally insured. Nobody ever got hurt. That was my number one rule. Nobody gets hurt. Only me. And I have paid my dues. And I accept responsibility for all my actions. No excuses.

Do I have any old scores to settle? For seven years I did. "Doogie." The RAT. The guy who set me up and tried to have me killed in the process so I would never return to haunt him.

For seven years I thought of little else: Revenge. He told the FBI. I wouldn't be taken alive and I would take as many as them with me as possible. Basically, that's a death warrant. And that's how they came. Prepared for a shoot-out. You know the story. And that was the most intense moment of my life. Not to mention the sense of betrayal I felt when I finally figured out who set me up and led me into the trap!

So for seven or eight or maybe nine years I thought of Doogie and what he did- until I just recently read this in "Cities of the Plains," by Cormac McCarthy. It's his third book of a trilogy, and it is as though this paragraph was written for me and I quote:

"He knew that our enemies by contrast seem always with us. The greater our hatred the more persistent the memory of them so that a truly terrible enemy becomes deathless. So that the man who has done you great injury or injustice makes himself a guest in your house forever. Perhaps only forgiveness can dislodge him."

Those are some pretty powerful words, and that's where I'm going to leave you hanging until the next time.

Mike

Reunion

"You will soon be with your family"

August 28, 2000

Dear Mike:

My entire family (45) went to Linda's parent's cabin near Zions National Park. It was the first Dwight Laws reunion. They have a basketball cement court. We played basketball (the serious contact version), vollyball, tetherball, and jump rope. Most of the kids had never jumped rope and they kept it going all day and night. I found a strategic chair and then grabbed kids as they came by and hugged them and then let them go. We had a carnival for all the kids with great prizes. By the end all the kids were walking around with bags full of stuff (28 grandchildren).

My engineering son gave teams of four a bag containing four straws, four toothpicks, four rubber bands, a tongue depressor, two paper plates, some string, wire twists, a pencil, rubber gum, four Styrofoam balls, a paper cup, and a sticker. Each team was to build a tower with a cup on top. Then the competition would include putting steel balls in the cup until the tower collapsed. A formula was devised to give more points for height then for weight—thereby encouraging height over shortness. For example, a twelve inch height that held four weights would not score as high as a 15 inch height with three weights. We had a blast. Some of the towers were symetric and beautiful. Others looked like a junk heap. The winner was a very ugly, cobbed together, structure. My team won the height contest but our tower collapsed before sufficient weight was added. My team took second place. It was interesting to see these teams, consisting of an old person, a young adult, a teenager, and a child, concentrate for hours on their design. Next to the jump rope competition the engineers tower was the second most popular event of the reunion.

* * * * * * * *

We went to a high mountain lake and baptized one of my granddaughters. It was a special event with everyone dressed in white. We also held church in the cabin.

I was particularly happy to participate in these events. I don't know when this cancer might get me so I have learned to enjoy every moment I can with my family.

* * * * * * * *

October 4th! Yahoo! Does that date still hold? Anymore exciting news? San Francisco huh? I am like your dad, scratching my head over that one. It is almost like they want you to fail—sending you right back into the heart of the problems. Oh well, anyone that has survived Lompoc can probably handle San Francisco. Just use your avoidance skills who have served you so well while you have been inside. When you arrive and get settled please call me at 1-800-468-4634 and let's talk. We need to start planning a 4X4 jeep trip to Southern Utah in the Spring, if you are able to come. I will cover all of the costs, food included. You just have to find a way to get here.

I loved your story about bringing the cops down on a drug exchange when they were looking for you. And the women at the bank coming to visit with you—incredible. You must have been some cool cookie. What would those women think if they ever knew they had spent the evening out the guy who robbed their bank? It is truly funny—well, as funny as a bank robbery can be.

Doogie? Hmmmmmm. That is tough for you. I am anxious to hear the continuing story in your next letter. I assume you have somehow dislodged him from your gut. I hope so. I have been thinking how much fun it would be for me to send him a letter (obviously I can't because I don't know where he lives) and tell him a good friend of mine has just been released from prison and would like to take him to lunch (perhaps a knuckle sandwich). Sorry! I'm not a good example when I talk like that. However, I still remember your capture story and I too had some strong feelings about Doogie. Maybe we should thank Doogie. Without him you might still be robbing banks, or worse yet, hurting someone, or be dead from drugs. You could go pin a rose on his nose that said, "I climbed out—you're still in the mire. Thanks, Doogie."

Michael, these are exciting times. Keep me posted.

Dwight

Ten Long Years

"I've been living the rich man's life."

September 21, 2000

Dear Dwight:

* * * * * * * *

My Mom put it all in perspective. She said, "You work out two hours a day. You study four hours. You take an afternoon siesta. In the real world, only rich people do that."

* * * * * * * *

You know sumpin'? She's got a point! It reminds me of the story of the native on the tropic island. He's swinging in a hammock, drinking lemonade in the shade, with a fishing line tied to his toe. Suddenly a large, very expensive yacht appears. The Captain, an elderly and grouchy man yells at the native (who's kicking back in the hammock) "Why don't you get a job?"
The natives' reply was, "Why?"
"So you can work all your life, then buy a boat like mine, and come to places like this and go fishing."

* * * * * * * *

A friend of my younger brother has offered me a job in construction. I don't know any of the details as of yet. But it's better to work for somebody who knows you as a person and not as an ex-con.

* * * * * * * *

Thanx for sharing your vacation/reunion with me. Sounds like you guys had a lot of fun!

* * * * * * * *

As soon as I get there I'll send you my new address and let you know how it is. I already know I'm going to experience some culture shock at first, but I adapt quickly, and am looking forward to breathing some fresh air. Change is good and I'm ready. Ten years is a long time.

* * * * * * *

Mike

Tasted a Sampling of Freedom

"And rejoiced!"

October 16, 2000

Dear Mike:

I have had this letter written and waiting to hear from you so I can post it to your new address. When I got news about your release and the details I think I was probably as excited as your other friends and family members. It was terrific. You have probably walked out on the street and tasted a sampling of freedom and rejoiced.

* * * * * * * *

I went riding last Friday (took a day off from work) and ended up over in Ely, Nevada. I camped at a KOA and enjoyed my new sleeping bag and tent. They all pack quite nicely on my motorcycle. As I was heading north the next day I got tired and decided to pick a spot to pull over and take a nap. As I approach a side road I hit some unexpectedly deep gravel and the motorcycle went out from under me and threw me into the gravel. My helmet protected me and my leathers also kept me from getting scrapes but I was so embarrassed that I jumped up to see if anyone had seen me. They hadn't. My bike is a new Valyrie (Honda) and has six cylinders. It is a monster, but sweet to ride. I was unable to lift it back up (650 lbs). After several attempts I had to flag down a motorist. He tried to keep the smile off his face as he helped me but I know he was telling a good story at the bar that evening.

* * * * * * * *

Dwight

Free at Last

"Don't fall out of your chair now, but Sunday I'm going to church."

October 27, 2000

Dear Dwight:

So much has happened I'm not sure where to start.

* * * * * * * *

I was a total basket case by the time I finally got to San Francisco International Airport. Everybody was there: Mom, Dad, David (my younger brother) with his wife and two kids I've never met until then. Little sister (Erin) was there with her two boys whom I've never met, and my son Jacob.

Dwight, I don't even know the words to describe how good that made me feel. That's the moment right then and there that convinced me never to commit another crime as long as I live.

* * * * * * * *

I hired on through the Union as a journeyman carpenter, so I'm making good money: $28.00 per hour and overtime and benefits. It's perfect. And I can practically walk to work, and check out all the little shops on the way. Big stores too! San Francisco is awesome. A nice place to visit.

* * * * * * * *

Don't have the time to run and work out like I used to. I raced a cable car one day from Market Street to Fishermans' Wharf. That was a good run! That was my first real taste of freedom. And I beat it by a mile!

* * * * * * * *

My first week I avoided work. Went out on "job search" every day but was dodging it. I needed a week just to come down. My feet weren't even toughing the ground. Then I went to the beach. Brought a lunch.

Wiggled my toes in the warm sand. Felt the ocean spray upon my smiling face and the answer came to me.

* * * * * * *

It was time to face reality. Vacation is over. Monday, find a job. Get a routine down and that's what I did. Followed my instruction. But never though I'd walk into a high-paying job. Somebody was looking out for me. And I thanked the Lord. And once again, my feet weren't even touching the ground.

* * * * * * *

Life is good.

Robbing the Robbers

"My friend "Scotty", an old lifer, who had quite a reputa-
tion in the Pen as one not to mess with, finally got out. Five
"punks" tried to rob him at the bus station. Little did
they know who they were messing with! He chased all five
of them down the street, demanding their money!"

November 21, 2000

Dear Dwight:

Time's flyin'... I forgot what a rat race the real world is; and people are oh so rude! But I'm enjoying it.

* * * * * * * *

My hours have been fluctuating drastically lately. When the concrete trucks roll in at 4:00 am, we have to be there. Which means I'm walking through the ghetto at 3:15am, when all the night people are still lurking in the shadows.

They've done everything from trying to sell me crack-cocaine, called me "cop", "white-boy", and one even tried to aggressively borrow $20.00. Remember that guy on the New York subway? Goetz? These young Black's tried to "aggressively borrow" $5.00 from him; he pulled out a gun and shot 'em all. Sometimes they leave you no other option. My life-skill instincts kicked in from the Penitentiary, and the panhandler sensed it. When he saw I was not intimidated by him he backed down.

* * * * * * * *

So my short term goal is to put as much money in the bank now as possible. [How ironic for a former bank robber.]

* * * * * * * *

You know something funny happened at the bank. I tried to open an account, *legally*. So I'm dealing with some lady with an attitude problem.

I'm trying to maintain my composure. She's resisting. The vault is open.
I'm looking at her. I'm looking at the vault. "Lady," I'm thinking, "If you
only knew. . ."

* * * * * * *

I know! Shame on me! But I wanted to show her how I open my
own account!

* * * * * * *

Mike

Drink Slowly My Friend

"They tells stories of the thirsty travelers who emerge from the desert and drink the cool fresh life saving waters with such uncontrolled desire that they kill themselves with the gourging."

December 16, 2000

Dear Mike:

Today I went down to the Bookstore and ordered your Christmas present. They told me they thought it would be sent directly to you in time for Christmas. Here's hoping. I am a little concerned because your last letter indicated you do not always get your mail. Keep an eye out for it and don't let your buddies get away with it. It is in a small box (about the size for a ring). The story that is depicted in your gift can be read about in the Book of Mormon, 1Nephi, chapter 8 and 11. Your gift is for Sundays and days off. Don't use it while doing construction.

* * * * * * * *

I thought I could deal with about anything, but I was wrong. The other day they told me I needed to climb in that MRI machine again.—you know, the one I call the sausage stuffer. Well, anyway, I went bonkers on them and wouldn't stay in the machine. They thought they had a crazy man on their hands. I stood up, put my clothes back on and walked out on them, climbed on my motorcycle and rode off down the street. I wonder if the insurance will pay the $1,000 for the time and machine. A costly waste I'm sure—but I just cracked. Enough is enough. I had laid in one of those machines for two hours a few days earlier for a Positron Emission Tomography (PET-scan). It showed that I have cancer in several places (metastatic disease). It's near my heart, under my tongue, adjacent to my spine, and in my throat. I guess my brain said, "Dwight, you can't stand any more of this probing." Anyway, I saw a lot of humor in it as well. Funny how people were suddenly tiptoeing around me. I thought of how the Indians are reported to have believed they should leave crazy people alone. I've learned something new. If I act crazy, I can get just about anything I want. No one is rude to me, and I can go anywhere with no interference. Wish I had known that forty years ago. Now my family is treating me with increased love, if that's possible, and I am the King. I tell ya human relations are an amazing phenomenon. There is one small thought that troubles me though. They say the crazy people don't think they're crazy. I'm acting crazy, but don't think I'm crazy. Does that mean I really am crazy?? Actually, I don't mind if I am crazy—just so I'm not stupid.

* * * * * * * *

My goodness. This last paragraph reads like it was written by a crazy man.

* * * * * * * *

I Love You
Dwight

Nobody Makes Eye Contact

"Big Cities are lonely."

[Mike sent three letters in a row.]

December 2000

Dear Dwight:

You should be receiving a little surprise package from Santa shortly hereafter. A very small token of my appreciation for everything you have done for me, and I will be <u>forever</u> grateful.

Dwight, life is good and getting better by the day. Don't have much of a social life though. Big cities are lonely. It's sad. Nobody makes eye contact. It's like they are afraid of something.

Work is going strong. It's the most money I've every made legally.

* * * * * * * *

Mike

December

Dear Dwight:

I don't know how you knew that I was looking for a ring and I don't know how you knew my size. But I guess it's not permitted to know all things. So I'll just thank you kindly. It's beautiful and I love it and have received several compliments already and I will cherish it forever.

I've read most of the story of Lehi. And will read it again before my next letter, which I intend to go into greater depth.

* * * * * * * *

Mike

Premonition

*"Half way through dinner I am over-
come with a terrible feeling of doom."*

January 22, 2001

Dear Dwight:

* * * * * * *

I was somewhat devastated by your most recent letter Dwight. I'm really truly and terribly sorry to have the sad news. It ain't right. You've done everything right and now this. That's something that happens to other people, not us! And now we are all afflicted. And I can't even begin to imagine what must be going through your mind. I tried to put myself in your shoes to see how I would react. My reactions were not positive at all. I admire your strength and courage Dwight. You have become quite an inspiration to me.

* * * * * * *

Six cylinders. My goodness, some cars don't have that much power! I guess that's a good way to deal with the pain. Ride hard. Ride fast.

* * * * * * *

They've laid off about two-thirds of the crew. I remain even though I was the last one hired. It's attitude. I show up every day. I'm first one there, last to leave. I work hard. Never complain. They're keeping me.

* * * * * * *

The strangest thing happened Wednesday. It was payday, so I treated myself to a steak dinner. Half way through dinner I am overcome with a terrible feeling of doom. I said things are going too good in my life that something terrible has to happen.

* * * * * * *

Until then, take care Dwight.

As always with the most profound respect
Your friend,
Mike

P.S. Did you ever receive the Ghirodelli chocolates I sent you?

Jeep Trip

"It is rated the number one jeep trail in the USA. My son has arranged for a camp cook to travel with us. All we do is drive and enjoy the scenery. They feed us and take great care of us. I have reserved a spot for you."

February 16, 2001

Dear Mike:

* * * * * * * *

I got on my horse, pictured below, and rode off. We went to Las Vegas, Needles, Blyth, Yuma, and finally into San Luis, Mexico. We then rode along the border to Sonoita, Mexico, then north into the USA again. We rode through the Organ Pipe Cactus National Monument, to Phoenix, to Kingman, across Hoover Dam, and back through Las Vegas to St. George, Utah. It was wonderful.

Now to some business. I have arranged a jeep trip into the confluence of the Colorado and San Juan Rivers. I have reserved a spot for you.

* * * * * * *

I will not accept "no" as an answer—well, I will.... but I won't like it.

* * * * * * *

My health is still unstable. My last surgery was tough but I am still going to work and doing my thing. They have decided radiation will not work, nor will chemo. So I just wait for the lumps to grow be enough and then they will perform surgery again. Whoooooeeeeh! In between surgeries I intend to put some miles on my bike. Beauty, ain't it. Yes sireeee! When you come up I'll let you take it for a spin. Only one rule—if you go over a hundred mph, don't let me see it.

Hang in there friend.
Dwight

Lunch in San Francisco

"He took me to see the building he is working on. They are making it earthquake proof. It was fascinating!"

April 19, 2001

I was in San Francisco so I contacted Mike and we meet at Fisherman's Wharf and I took him to lunch. We laughed and visited for an hour or two and then he had to leave. He showed me the new pickup he had purchased. He was proud of it. He drove off to cross the Golden Gate Bridge on his way home.

He is coming for the jeep trip. Yahoooo!

Charged Up

"We can talk more when you get here but I just wanted to get you excited with these pictures."

May 11, 2001

Dear Mike:

* * * * * * * *

I was so excited to have dinner with you in San Francisco. The tour of your building and the work you are doing was very interesting. I am particular pleased you are going to try and come for the September 4X4 trip.

* * * * * * * *

Here are some shots of my son's previous trips

* * * * * * * *

* * * * * * *

That ought to be enough to get you excited for the trip. You probably don't want to try this with your new pickup. It is a beauty

Dwight

I'm In

"The good news is my parole officer has given me an unofficial "yes" on my (our) planned trip to Utah in September."

June 16, 2001

Dear Dwight:

* * * * * * *

I want to thank you for the wonderful time we spent together in San Francisco. I would not have missed it for anything in the world.

* * * * * * *

She (my parole officer) wants a letter from you describing the situation/scenario. In other words, she wants it in your words what the trip will encompass. [Mike told me by telephone she was concerned if we started drinking. Hah!]

* * * * * * *

Mike

Dear Parole Officer

"We take out only memories and leave only footprints."

July 11, 2001

Dear Officer Magnasco:

This September my son and I are taking approximately Forty people on a three day adventure into the red rock wilderness of Southern Utah (near the confluence of the San Juan and Colorado arms of Lake Powell). It is a 4-wheel trip. The road is extremely rough and major 4-wheeling occurs. We have taken this group for several years and the trip has been fascinating, exhilarating, and just plan fun. The participants are associates of my son (mostly engineers), and me (mostly educators). Some bring their families and some come solo. We have strict rules for the group. No off road riding to damage the environment, no hot-dogging or unreasonable risk-taking, absolutely no alcohol, no smoking, and no drugs. Actually, most of the participants are non-drinkers/smokers anyway. The group begins and ends the day with prayer.

The previous groups have enjoyed lots of fun and fellowship. We hire a cook. We ride in to a camp site the first night. The cook feeds us dinner and then breakfast the following day. We 4-wheel into the confluence and then back out to the camp for the second night. The cook takes care of us again. Then the third day we ride back out. We haul our own water and food in, and our trash out. We take out only memories and leave only footprints.

I have asked Michael Taylor to join our group. Hopefully, you will approve that request.

Call me at (801) 378-7224 if you have any additional questions. Michael will ride with me and another one of my sons in our jeep.

Thank you for this consideration.

Dwight Laws

Approved

"She likes me."

August 14, 2001

Dear Dwight:

* * * * * * *

Rest assured that I will be there in September. Christine (my Parole officer) has approved it.

* * * * * * *

Send me details.

Mike

Family Member

"They're all anxious to meet you—you are famous with them.
For six years I've told them about you. They
think you are a family member."

August 20, 2001

Dear Mike:

Glad to get the positive confirmation. I am excited. Yahoo! We will leave very early on the 20th of September from my house (maybe by 5am). Come and stay with us the night before (maps enclosed). Bring a sleeping bag and tent in case of rain. Enclosed are the sheets we sent to everyone. Your fee is already paid. All you need to worry about is getting to Provo. Ride with us the rest of the way (or take your truck as far as Calvin Black Memorial airport).

If you can arrive by 6 or 7pm on the night of the 19th I would love to have a little barbecue and introduce you to some of my family members.

* * * * * * * *

Dwight

Party At The Park

"Michael arrived at 6pm this evening in his pickup.
The whole family was there to meet him and we went
across the street and had a party in the park."

Michael   Ryan (my son)   Dwight

September 19, 2001

The morning of the 20th we left on our trip. We went to the south side of Hole-in-the-Rock. We had a glorious day of jeeping and talking and jeeping and eating and jeeping and sightseeing. Mike drove the jeeps and loved it. He swam in the Colorado arm of Lake Powell near the Rincon and was like a little kid.

At one of the most beautiful spots on the trip I had this picture taken with Michael.

It was a glorious trip – for both of us.

Dwight   &   Michael

Where Are You?

*"After our wonderful trip we agreed that we didn't
need to write so often. He now has a life."*

May 3, 2002

Dear Mike

Are you trying to hide? Where are you? I guess if you are not going to write me and give me your new address I'll have to wake up your mother at 6am (oops!) and get it from her.

* * * * * * * *

Your mom says you are still working hard—real hard. Doesn't surprise me.

* * * * * * * *

Mike, I'm concerned about you. I know you are working hard, but I also know how difficult it is on the outside with relationships, bills, being self organized (rather than only responding), making decisions about life style, religion, politics etc. Take a moment and write me one of those thoughtful letters you used to write from "the place."

I love you
Dwight

Feeling of Doom
(personal thoughts)

*"I got nervous when I didn't hear from him. I recalled he had
promised that no one was out to settle a score, but I couldn't
shake my foreboding, especially since he had confessed to me
the experience of suddenly having a feeling of doom."*

Summer of 2003

*"I wonder if he is getting into mischief and doesn't want to correspond with
me?"*
Summer of 2004

*"My life has been totally consumed with my cancer, surgeries, and other family
matters, but I still think of you, Michael. I don't have your address so please
write to me."*
Summer of 2005

*"I decided I had to know how you were. So I called your mother. She was not
in but I left a message. I told her I hadn't heard from you for a couple of years
and I wanted to know where you were and what you were doing."*
April 28, 2006

No! Please, No!

"The following is written in my journal."

It finally reached the point that I wouldn't wait any longer. Friday morning I got on the phone and called Mike's parents in Winters, California. I hadn't heard from him in over two years. After our great jeep trip to Southern Utah I thought we had become fast friends. When he returned to his job in San Francisco, I heard from him a couple of times and then he stopped responding to me. I tried to contact him several times but he dropped me cold. I wanted his parents to update me on where I could find him.

I got an answering service when I called the Taylors.

"Please leave a message."

"Hi. This is Dwight Laws, Mike's Friend. I am the one who wrote to him over an eight year period while he was in jail. I haven't heard from him in a couple of years and would very much like to see how he is doing and get in touch again. You can reach me on my cell phone at 801 368 5297. Thank you very much."

After leaving the message I was soon involved in work again and gave it no further thought.

Saturday I spent the day with my grandchildren who were living with us for a couple of days while their apartment was becoming available.

Sunday, April 30, 2006 they went to church with us and then we had a lovely dinner at our home. After dinner we sat visiting and enjoying one another's company. In the midst of the conversation my cell phone rang. I answered it while the rest of the family continued jabbering.

"Hello."

"Is this Dwight Laws?"

"Yes."

"This is (couldn't understand the first name) Taylor."

I didn't know who it was or what it was about. Before I could ask for more information she said, "We are from Winters California and you called to ask about our son."

I was very excited. This was the call I was waiting for.

"Yes, I'm thank you for calling. I haven't heard from Mike for a long time I'm excited to catch up with him and see how he is doing. He kept in touch with me after our trip but suddenly I didn't hear from him again."

There is silence on the other end and I somehow understood she was silently sobbing. Then she forced herself to speak. "Come this June 08, he will have been buried for two years."

I was thunderstruck! Before I could fashion a proper response she continued.

"He went to visit his brother in Oregon. He left his brother one day, saying he was going out to make a call, and disappeared.

My mind was racing.

"Five months later they found his body in a field in Oregon. It was badly decomposed."

It was painful to hear such a report about someone I had invested so much time and effort in.

"He had been shot in the head."

I was stunned!

Linda saw the expression on my face and she stopped talking. Of course she was afraid my reaction must be related to someone in our own family. I mouthed the words to her, "It's Mike Taylor's parents", so she wouldn't panic. But she knew something was wrong.

I can't remember what words of comfort I may or may not have responded with. I tried to tell her how sorry I was and how highly I thought of him.

"We have no idea how it happened, who did it, why it happened. . . . he had so many demons—they finally caught up with him." She sobbed again. She then tried to thank me for being the only person outside of her and her husband who had shown him any love or affection in his whole life. I can't remember how the conversation terminated—but I do know I didn't sleep much that night.

The following day I called Steven Walker to tell him what happened. Steven is an English professor at Brigham Young University who had helped me try and publish some of Mike's story with Deseret Book two years before. Although the submission was rejected, Steve had become fond of Mike through this process even though he never met him. Steven told me he, like me, was stunned at the news. We talked for a while and then he said, "Dwight, I've don't usually say things like this, but. . . .I love you." Our experience of trying to bring Mike's story together had also brought us very close together.

Two of my work associates, Haws Marble, and Debbie Taylor (no relation) had been on the trip to Southern Utah and also became friends with Mike. I told each of them what had happened and they were both saddened by the news.

Terry Summerhays had also been on that trip. He came to Provo to give my son a vocal lesson last night and I told him about Mike. We talked about Mike and everlasting outcomes and mercies and the grace of God.

I must say this affected me more than I might have imagined, as if I had lost a family member.

A Mother's Broken Heart

"I sent Mike's mother copies of our correspondence after I heard of his passing. I hoped they would be comforting."

June 24, 2006

Dear Dwight:

I apologize for my procrastination in acknowledging your package.

There are a couple of reasons for this; my limited abilities and of course the subject of Mike.

Multiple times I have composed this letter in my mind and I must now write a few of my thoughts down on paper.

About halfway through your collection of letters, I found I was unable to continue to read further. Even though much of what he wrote, he had already shared with us, I began to wonder if I had the right to read that which wasn't written to us personally. Is it an invasion? Someday I may be able to again pick them up and finish reading his letters.

Michael, under a controlled environment, excelled.

I know his correspondence with you, elevated him to greater heights and greater challenges. You encouraged him, helped him and befriended him. He believed you cared.

When he was doing so well with his studies, had goals, I dared to hope 'again.'

I prayed for Michael's mortal soul in life and I pray for his mortal soul in death.

When Michael was given his freedom, he tried very hard. He found a good job which had very good pay. He worked very hard, maybe too hard. He could be intense. It was more than he could cope with. The everyday challenges of life were too hard, and finally the dark side of Mike and his demons won out.

We grieve our lose. We grieve for him because it was such a waste of a life. He had so much potential.

He had our love and love of many others. Mike was encouraged and helped along the way. He is missed.

I pray he knows this even now. He is in the Lord's loving hands. Thank you for your many kindnesses.

He died on February 8, 2004. We buried him on June 29, 2004.

Respectfully yours,
Cynthia Taylor

THE END

About the Author

Dwight and Linda Laws are the parents of nine children, thirty-seven grandchildren, and two great-grandchildren. Dwight earned his doctorate in Instructional Science and Technology from Brigham Young University and for the past twenty years has directed the nation's largest distance education program. He was raised as a member of the Church of Jesus Christ of Latter-day Saints and was taught to believe in and look for the goodness of humanity. He has worked for two different international airlines and has been able to travel the world. His international travels opened his eyes to countries, cultures, and wonderful people. However, Dwight discovered a unique nation of the world, one that lives behind bars. The culture of those who are incarcerated is grim, often evil, and mostly forgotten. Yet, even here, Dwight found wonderful people. This story is about the incredible life of one of these people.

www.ingramcontent.com/pod-product-compliance
Lightning Source LLC
Chambersburg PA
CBHW021559280526

45784CB00001BA/426